Reflexions

Stories & Poems by Tony DePaul

Published (2018) by Agreement with
Summerfield Publishing/
d.b.a. New Plains Press
216 South 8th Street
Suite 105
Opelika, AL, 36801

Printed in the United States of America.

LIBRARY OF CONGRESS
CATALOGING-IN-PUBLICATION DATA
Categories: American Poetry, Philadelphia Poetry, Chestnut Hill
Poetry, short short stories, Poetry collection, Short story collec-
tion, Existential poetry, Deistic literature, dramatic stories.

Library of Congress Control Number
2018954283

ISBN13: 9780998685731

DePaul, Anthony 1944 –

This is a work of fiction, and any resemblances between the stories, settings, and characters to any real people, places, or events
is, well, fiction.

Table of Contents

Foreword

Reflexions is a collection of poetry and short fiction, singular expressions of pain, love, grief, salvation, and betrayal. The book poses moral questions amid tangible, vivid images, and draws the reader into a world at once Existential, Deistic, and dramatic, and unforgettable.

It is a journey of many souls on many treks leading to a common path to truth.

Prologue

It is impossible to say exactly what I feel.
It is impossible to know all I want to say.
The only possibility is to keep talking
Until the truth speaks from me.

On Being an Eagle

The eagle climbed high to meet the geese,
All brown and squawking and fixed in a vee
Against the sky. "Ah, here is place," cried the bird.
"Belonging, and a course to fly."
But geese go only north or south
Without Will. Eagles need space and thought.
And so the eagle broke off and flew
Alone as eagles should, without a sound.
Turning and turning ever upward
The Eagle soared, wings unbent
Stretched in a broad, unyielding arc
Spiraling toward the power of the sun,
Higher and higher, then gone
Amid blazing light
Fused in radiance
Beyond eyes and Thought.

Epiphany

November closed on me, icing me,
Cold places. No words or images came
To mind, no thoughts jumped with life
And I, a poet, felt shame.

My spirit dry as dying leaves,
I opened the door, ran fearful
Alone to the woods and walked beneath
Dark trees. My body and spirit spent.

I stretched out crying on the hard earth,
Afraid of dying before my death
Afraid of a night without morning light,
Afraid of taking another breath.

Suddenly the sky exploded. The sun,
Burning a fiery red, flood,
Shot like lightning through the trees
And roasted my cold, still blood.

I stopped crying and looked with wonder
As dying leaves brightened to life
Shining in the death throes of winter,
Radiant under the brilliant sunlight.

I smiled, then laughed, drunk with life,
Suspended near its wild heart,
At one with the sky, leaves, trees,
Now a whole, fused into one image.
But clouds moved, blocking the sun

The light faded, the leaves descendedBrittle,
wrinkled, dusty with death.
The candle spent, the moment ended.

And so I left the dark, cold woods
Shivering, I yearned for paper and pen,
A child reborn to the whole of life,
A man in love with beauty again.

The Hidden Muse

A sad song touches me, simple lyrics straining
Against the winds of past loneliness, sorrows
From another time and planet, another age
When the fever to create raced in my veins.

The call from afar, seizes the fearful moment
Icing truth inside an igloo under a cold sun
Bright, lightning flashing across a frozen pond
A crystal image, a pang of truth, calling me.

So I write in a heartfelt stream of new images,
Penning images as VIVID as a lover's cry
Piercing darkness, a red-hot moment of ecstasy
Shouted from the core of a lover to a lover.

Do I dare walk among oft friendly trees
Or skip stones across the endless creek
Or sip wine and listen to Dylan or Bocelli
Lest the muse leap alive and waken me to write?

Mr. Mortality

The scoundrel Death shadows me daily, hourly, now
Like a burglar crouching behind the drapes
Ready to spring on me. Bang I am dead.
Bang I am in heaven, bang I am in Hell.

Or Death teases me, nearly taking me
In car accidents, feverish flus, disease,
A crab scratching my heart's lining,
Gray smoke gnawing my lungs and throat.

He strangles my relatives and friends,
Searing them in cancerous sores,
In wracking rasps, in piercing pain
In spasms, strokes, and fatal falls.

I fear him not, now nor never.
I respect his power not his duty.
I stand up and hold my ground
My middle finger upright and firm.

My mortality is certain but not fatal.
My blood flows in my child's veins.
I shall live beyond this life and will laugh last
At death's feeble efforts to destroy me.

The Smiling Child

She walked, striding, against the virus
The illness tilting her left eye aside
The villain restraining her growth,
Her mind set to conquer, to achieve.

Her courage twinkles in her eyes
Lighting the room, the hearts of parents
Grandparents, brother and nurses, doctors
Amazed, in awe, grateful, hopeful.

And then she smiles from chin to cheeks to head
As though to calm our fears, assure us
She is well and thriving, alert, happy.
Ready to earn her place in her world.

A child leading her family forward
Renewing our faith and strength, charging
Onward, one step, then another, again
Uplifting all spirits with her constant smile.

Betrayals

They dwelled under my skin
Parasites munching my organs–
I craved their love, trusted them
Unqualified, blind love and faith.

Lies hidden in smiles, Family, Friends,
 Children, parents, siblings, workers
Sub rosa, stabbing, cutting with glee
They wrapped my kindness in scorn.

They spread their gossip and lies
In emails, Facebook, tweets, phone calls,
In whispers, in phony praise, laughing aside,
Duping a good and generous man.

But I learned the truth, facing spite,
Evil guised as love and respect,
I shed them, cleansing my soul,
Clearing my way to live with the TRUTH.

Humility replaced vanity, courage replaced need,
New love, new life, new will to move ahead with grace,
Through honesty, true friends, and LOVE,
Hope in living without liars and traitors.

Peter and the Rose

Peter had a secret garden, a small plot of azaleas, violets, mums, geraniums, and roses tucked away in the woods of Fairmount Park, a mile from his home. He liked the rich hues and vibrant expressions of nature in bloom. He worked the garden alone, careful that his buddies would not see his softer side.

A forty-five-year-old man should not be sensitive to any childish jibes about his masculinity. He'd fathered four sons, strong athletic boys who looked up to him as the rock of their family. Someday he'd take the newborn grand children here but for now it was best to keep his love of flowers to himself.

He excluded his wife Marge from his garden. She would not understand why anything other than she was worthy of Peter's attention. She had her world of cooking, tennis, bridge, and casinos. He had the flowers.

One day he strolled along a wooded path in Fairmount Park to the garden, whistling a song he'd imagined as a boy. He'd never put words to the song. He just liked the tune and melody and the fact that he alone owned it. The melody was his unique signal to a world deaf to his voice.

A Boy Scout troop approached him, marching in single file, their faces stern, unsmiling. They should be happy, he thought. The Scoutmaster was a hulk of a man with shoulders as wide as a buck's antlers.

"Morning, Sir," said the Scoutmaster.

"Morning, Sir," echoed his charges in unison.

"Good morning to all," said Peter. Too grim by half.

He paused until they turned the bend of the path. He headed toward the garden, trudging on fronds and avoiding the poison ivy, freshly sprouted and ready to slap an itch on him.

As he neared the shining mums, violets and gardenias, a flash of brilliant red caught his eye. To his amazement, a single crimson rose peered up at him. His heart jumped two beats. How beautiful

21

and unexpected.

He stared at the rose for a long moment, savoring its lush splendor. It outshone all of his flowers. He had to have it.

He kept his garden tools in a waterproof chest hidden in the hollowed-out center of a huge oak tree. Quickly, he dug around the rose, careful not to cut its roots. There were no thorns, just tiny green buds winking from the stem.

He planted the rose in the center of the garden, feeling lucky and proud of his newly found gem. The flower glowed as if smiling at its new owner. The flower had a singular presence among the other flowers. It was a god-sent prize.

For a month Peter tended to the rose, feeling an attachment to the red petals arching in the radiant sun. He textured the ground with treated soil to nourish it.

Dark green buds opened as tiny pin-like thorns emerged and grew into nasty-looking needles. Peter ignored the sharp needles, thinking only of the rose, his special flower.

Another month passed and the rose kept its luster. The thorns sprouted all along the stem in prickly branches, crisscrossing the red petals.

Peter carefully poked his fore finger through the thorns to touch the petals. He caressed the rose petals, so soft, so lustrous.

As he took his finger away, he scratched it against a thorn. A tiny dot of blood oozed from his skin as if he had paid a toll to touch the rose. The prick hurt so he sucked the wound. The red dot of blood stopped but then slowly popped out of his skin like a pimple.

"Damn."

The leaves behind him rustled. Startled, he nearly fell at the sight of the buck, his twelve-point antlers held high like a king's crown. The buck sniffed the trees and then the ferns and plants. He chewed up a gaggle of weeds, lifting his head up afterwards as if to announce that he was ready to devour the woods in one ravenous feast. The buck lowered his nose to the garden. Peter grabbed a gardening spade from his tools.

"Away. Get away," he shouted.

The buck stepped back but did not bolt. A doe would bolt. A fawn would scamper away. But a buck was not so easily chased from a meal of flowers.

The buck thrust its nose towards the rose flush into the thorns.

Peter readied his best baseball swing, but the thorns eerily seemed to attack the buck's nose and cheeks as if they were a boxer punching in a flurry. Blood oozed out. The buck reared away, surging through the trees to safety. Peter knelt on one knee like an altar boy genuflecting at Mass.

"Thank god for thorns. Beauty must be protected," Peter said aloud.

The forest could take the garden but not the rose. The rose was special.

He visited the rose every day after dinner.

"I am walking to lose weight," he told his wife.

As summer approached, the rose thrived, shining in a sweet splendor among the other flowers that Peter barely attended. He thought of extracting the rose to create a garden of one. A rose garden like the White House. Yes. Someday soon he would enshrine the rose.

He visited the rose on a late August day at dusk. As he rounded the bend, whistling, he smelled the smoke of a campfire. The smoke fluttered above the garden as the Boy Scouts sat around the campfire roasting marshmallows. Each boy had a flower from the garden pinned to his chest: gardenias, mums, and violets. Frantically, he raced from boy to boy looking for the rose.

"Where is my rose?"

The Scoutmaster marched up to him. The Scoutmaster's eyes belied his guilt.

"Was that your garden we found? We had no idea anyone would cultivate a garden in a forest. We assumed it was a leftover nature project. Besides, the flowers were not well attended. They were unpruned and just not cared for. So we took them as prizes. We meant no harm."

Peter thrashed among the boys. "Who has the rose? Give it up or I swear I will kick everyone's ass. It is my rose and I want it. Where is it? Come on you twerps. Where is my rose?"

The Scoutmaster motioned to the boys to back away. "Relax scouts. The gentleman is upset. Now, did anyone see a rose among the flowers? Come on, fess up. Who has the rose?"

Silence.

Peter raced to the tool area. He cocked the garden shovel high above the heads of the scouts.

"I will use this garden shovel on all of you, unless you give me my rose back," said Peter.

"Whoa, Mister. Steady. These boys did nothing wrong. They certainly do not need to be threatened over a single rose."

"It's not any rose. It is my rose. The most beautiful rose in God's creation. I want it back."

"Okay. We will look for it. Boys, uh, scatter and look for the rose. Do as I say. Scatter now!"

The scouts took off running in all directions. The scoutmaster edged away.

"Look Mister. Those boys are innocent. They did not destroy or steal your rose. Nor did I. You are upset. Here. Put down the shovel. I'll get you a marshmallow on a stick. Ah, here's one. It's charred a bit but still tasty. Have a bite."

Peter's chest heaved from a pain inside his heart. Tears welled up in his eyes. "You damn fool. You don't understand that you killed something beautiful. That is the greatest of all sins. Murder of beauty, murder of truth, murder of life itself. Murder me. Yes, you murdered me."

"You are not well, my friend. I am leaving you to search for your rose. I hope you find it."

The Scoutmaster backed away then turned and ran, leaving Peter shivering in pain under the setting sun.

"Murderers all," said Peter, meaning Marge and his sons and his buddies and the deer and the scouts.

He sat by the fire crying until he fell asleep like a lost and abandoned child rolled up in a fetal position, alone in a dark place, dreaming of a rose.

The Uber Ride

The blizzard of 2016 blanketed the Philly area in a vise-like freeze. For two days nobody moved from their homes. We were all resigned to the white prison of a winter cold. Cabin fever set in by Monday, so at nine a.m. I pressed my Uber online button. I had to get out to the real world and drive.

My wife of forty-one years sat across the kitchen table. Rosemary O'Toole had married me over the objections of her sainted Irish Catholic parents. She still looked pretty to me. Her freckles kept her looking like a schoolgirl.

"John, we need milk but I don't want you going out until the plows are done."

"They were done an hour ago. I like doing Uber."

"It's dangerous."

"Ah, only pros like me are out today."

"You are one stubborn dago."

"Yes I am." I pressed the Uber icon on my iPhone.

Three minutes later, the iPhone buzzed. I did not bother to check the pick-up location. I was so anxious to escape.

"Where are you going?"

"Out."

Six minutes later I picked up three black boys around 9:30. Two piled into the back seat, while a giant of a boy plopped his six-foot eight frame in the bucket seat next to me. His jean-clad knees hunched against the dashboard.

"Norristown High School is our destination. Right?" I asked.

"You got it, Mister John. I am Darryl and back there is Cody, and the dude with the goatee that looks like a rat's ass is Moe."

Darryl turned to me. Sitting down he was a foot taller than me.

"First we stop at Wawa. I needs to eat. Hey Mister Johnny. You look sharp in that Stetson hat. What you want for it?"

"It's a gift, so it's not for sale," I said.

"Turn on station 99.7," said Moe from the back seat. "I gotta have some hip hop to wake my ass up."

I turned it on and headed to the Wawa on Whitehall Road a quarter mile from the high school. The boys thanked me and chatted up music.

They beat rhythm in their sing along while I tried hard to shut out the profane lyrics. Darryl nudged me, a friendly elbow suggesting a strong but friendly physical force. He was not trying to intimidate me.

He stared down on me, smiling. "Mister Johnny, what would you do if Beyonce sat on your face?"

"Have an early dinner," I said.

The boys all howled.

Darryl laughed so hard his head jerked back showing a toothy smile spread across his handsome face and bushy mustache.

"Damn, Mister Johnny. You quick. Riddle me this. How many ways can you do a woman in thirty seconds?"

I hesitated for about ten seconds as if I was doing a math problem.

"Five ways."

"Five ways?

What five ways?"

"Missionary, doggy, side, sittin–up, and upside down."

The car exploded in laughter. "Damn. We got the coolest Uber dude on the planet," said the other back seater.

"What you do to Beyonce's hair while you puttin' the wood to her?" asked Cody.

"I get her to tie it in pigtails then I hold on for the ride."
More laughter.

"My man John thinks he's John Wayne," said Darryl tearing in laughter.

"Johnny, Johnny. What if old Bernie Mack snuck up behind you while you were doing Beyonce. What would you do?" asked a boy in the back seat.

Caught up in the moment, I answered quickly, way too quickly. "Shoot his balls off."

Hands clapping. Laughter.

"Damn. John is stone cold. A real man," said Darryl.

I wanted to grab back the words but the moment was gone.

My stomach sunk in embarrassment and shame. I owed them a decent answer, not the words of a street punk. I failed them. They needed a straight answer and I'd fed them punk talk.

We reached the Wawa. They clambered inside while I thought how to get straight with them. No words came. I was as blind as a fly in the blizzard. So the boys came back with breakfast sandwiches and coffee. Darryl unwrapped a bagel loaded with eggs and cheese. "Want a bite?"

"I'm good," I said.

"I'm gettin' me an AR 25," said Darryl.

"Me too," said the other boys in unison.

For the next two minutes, they talked about owning guns as easily as if they were talking about basketball or women. Guns were natural to them. Too natural. I owned a twenty-two rifle when I was seventeen. I bought it to protect my family. These kids did it to prove their manhood. My heart sank again. I had sent them the wrong message. What could I say to help them? A minute later, I parked the car at the rear door to the high school. The brown brick building looked ominous and anonymous. A book without words.

"Hey, Mister Johnny. You are a handsome dude and cool as snow. Come on in with us. Everybody would like you. You'd be the Principal by lunch time," said Darryl.

He meant it. But I could not go to his world. I could not weather his storm.

"Can't do it guys. Thanks for riding with me."

Darryl tapped his fist on my shoulder. "Stay cool my man."

I looked away as they walked to the school to finish the next day in their lives. Sad as a damp day, I drove to the end of the parking lot and switched my iPhone to "On Line," and I rated the boys "five stars."

Those boys needed a leader, a mentor, a father, a grandfather, a priest to cut down the evil vines of the culture in which they were raised. It held them in twisted handcuffs. By talking trash and sounding "cool," as the hip hop lyrics, I had given them tacit approval of a culture that could doom them.

God, please help them. They need guidance not laws. They need a GPS to sanity and goodness. Somebody help them before they kill each other to be a man.

I drove away very slowly, haunted by the legacy of the ride.

They deserved a better driver.

The windshield wipers brushed away the new snow but my eyes were too soggy to see the road ahead. In the rear-view mirror, the school faded from view, wrapped in the mist of winter.

The iPhone buzzed me for a pick up. I pressed the black figure on the iPhone 6 Screen.

I got home by noon, milk in hand. Rosemary met me with her best nun-like frown.

"I was scared skinny. The news showed a dozen accidents. It's dangerous out there. Stay home please."

I patted her thinning hair. "Why do you still act like you are my mother?"

"Don't be stubborn. Come and eat lunch and we'll play hand and foot."

I wanted to tell her about the boys. They needed parenting. They were in danger, not me. "Sure Rosemary. I'll rest up. Driving can be a real challenge. You never know what roads you travel even with a GPS."

"Sit. I'll make you coffee."

"Coffee would be nice."

She kissed my cheek. "Stop driving in the snow. Promise?"

I squeezed her hand realizing just how lucky I was to not need a gun to be a man.

The IRDGADs

*F*riday, November 23rd, 1963, 2:30 PM, we walked out of La-Salle's College Hall on to Olney Avenue. The guys had early classes so they wanted me to cut my afternoon class and drink beer while they played basketball. Our intramural team had lost every game thereby honoring our team acronym- IRDGAD–I really don't give a damn.

The whole campus, including the Christian Brothers who ran the School, knew what the letters stood for. Called on the carpet by Brother Gavin who was VP of student affairs, meaning a disciplinarian, I declared the D stood for DARN which is an accepted word. Brother Gavin laughed at my explanation but went along with the story.

Practice was futile since we could shoot, pass, dribble, or even call timeouts properly. Besides, I was still wearing a brace around my stomach. My appendicitis had burst inside my flat iron stomach and I survived the ensuing deadly peritonitis infection. But I had 88 stitches inside and 23 outside. A zipper ran from my belly button to my crotch. So, I was wearing a "girdle" to keep my guts in place. Death and I had shaken hands.

As we emerged from College Hall, a radio report from a car parked at the curb blurted that JFK was dead, killed in Dallas by an assassin. Shocked, we piled into the car scarcely able to talk. We rode home craving beer and the solace of each other's friendship. We needed to bond to keep our minds in some semblance of sanity. JFK was a god to us, a reincarnation of hope and civility. He died before we reached home.

Two days later, five of us drove to DC to pay our respects. There was Skippy, Jimmy O, Dave, Tommy, and I huddled into a cramped old Chevy. We barely had gas money. We reached DC and parked as close as we could to the funeral line. Among a cordon of people, silent, heads bowed, we walked solemnly past our dead hero. None of us said much. Our mutual sadness and grief made words useless.

That day changed our world and in me heightened my awareness of life's fragility and value.

I lived in a hurry, anxious to suck up every aspect of life. My internal clock ran 24 hours a day. My mind raced on. I read books, watched old and new movies, trying to memorize each scene as if I would never see them again. The clock ticked too fast. Life was soooooo short. I wanted to devour it before death closed on me like a stage curtain on a play.

Skippy died first in a car accident on April fool's night, 1972. An old woman veered out of her lane and sent his VW bug into oncoming traffic. The impact crushed his chest into his heart. He was 27 with a baby girl and wife.

The day before he told me he was finally getting a hold of himself and his life. His dreams lay crushed in that car. I wrote two poems about him. We buried him with some words of his favorite writer, Kahlil Gabrin, emblazoned on his grave stone.

A couple of years later, Jimmy O died from lung cancer. Oddly, the man did not smoke. Jimmy had the Irish wit of a Johnathan Winters. He could snap off one liners and do imitations that made a room collapse into laughter. The last time I saw him he had a "WHY ME" look of bewilderment on that once happy face.

Esophageal cancer took Dave in his early sixties. Dave was a physically and mentally strong man. He fought cancer to the end, never complaining. He died with dignity.

Tommy buried his beloved wife Regina who succumbed to breast cancer after a long battle. A year later, Tommy went to sleep after breakfast at the shore and never woke up. He needed to see Regina.

We all shared a kindred spirit, a brotherhood. JFK would have liked having a beer with us. In his honor, we changed IRDGAD to mean–I really do give a damn.

"Tap a fresh keg boys. I will be joining you and Jack K."

To Skip–One Year Later

The Earth did not quake when you died,
The moon and stars held their place.
The sun rose brightly the next morn,
Life sprinted onward like a race horse.

The April flowers budded ripely,
The grass grew greener and stronger
As Spring leaped alive, bounding
Each day lasting longer.

They buried you in fertile ground
Beneath tall, healthy oaks
That swayed ever so softly,
Gently rocked by warm breezes.

You would have loved the day after
The night they killed you, brother.
We would have laughed and drank wine
And lived that day like all the others.

But night closed on you
Amid the crash of metal and glass,
Crushing flesh and bloody bones
In one fatal, fated pass.

Your body and my soul broke.
Your heart and my soul bled,
Your eyes and my soul closed.
You and I share death, forever.

A Death on my Vacation

Seashells blue and black
Empty, colorless and cracked
In two by the surging surf.

Souvenirs and sailor hats
Scenic mugs and place mats
In boardwalk shops and stands.

Misty melting gray metal sky
Dull. Lifeless air of clay,
A blanket over sand and sea.

Spin the wheel and win the prize
One quarter buys you three tries,
For teddy bears and gingham cats.

Children, chilled, iced in the sun,
Cold Shivering all as one,
In circles shaking without sound.

Hot dogs, pizza, water ice,
Children laughing; it's so nice,
To ride a Ferris wheel.

Angry water green and white,
Wild currents clinging tight,
Until a child yields and drowns.

No more rides and candy today.
Tomorrow brings another day
Of life and games for us to play.

Friends and Lovers in Life and Death

I Miss
The touch of one gentle hand
On the tender lining of my soul.

The glint of knowing eyes
Lighting the shadows of my mind.

The nights of wine-filled laughter
The music that beat savage rhythms.

The moments of melting love
When two lives became one.

I Remember
The grace of loving another
More than loving myself.

The solace of friendship
From the trials we shared.

The days of bright sunshine
On the beaches of our youth.

The moment of death
When two lives became one.

Requiescat da Mater

They told me it was for the best
Pain can only be soothed by death
Life can find but one place to rest.

They told me time would ease my sorrow
Wounds of loss will quickly heal
Surely, I'd be better tomorrow.

They told me God had taken her
Heaven's her just reward
She'd be happy with her maker.

But on that cold day I laid her down
Kneeling, drenched in stinging, icy rain
Genuflected, and bent, facing the ground, and

I told myself she wasn't gone
She lived inside of me, not in heaven, and
love doesn't die, it just passes on

From life to life, from her to me,
Her child today, her child tomorrow.
Blood of her blood, body of her body.

"Do I dare to eat a peach?"
– Prufrock

Hamlet sat and waited for himself
To act, then died trying to act.
His immobility was imbecility
Disguised as ambiguity.

His incapacity for capacity
Strangled his will to win
His death was ineluctable
The cowardice of mental fatigue.

Fear of not knowing freezes a man,
Ices his courage in stark safety
Excuses his lack of action;
He's one of the boys.

Huddled around low fires
Singing Home on the range
Roasting Marshmallows
Afraid of the dark.

So, a scared man does not grab
His life by its throat or balls
Instead he scratches his ass
Till the last darkness falls.

The Camping Trip

Come sit around the fire
My children, close to the light.
Let me see your bright young faces
Glow warm and red tonight.

Let me see your fair hair glisten
The flames dancing in your eyes
Little tongues of fire
Licking the whites of your eyes.

For now I am an old man
And I need the coming sleep
I need to lie in a cradle
And rock and rock to sleep.

So, before I close my eyes
One last look at life I need
To remember I created love
And not hate and pride and greed.

Portrait of La Bella Femina

She leapt into my life like a new born child
Surprising, aglow, haloed in sunlight
Her eyes struck mine, piercing the dark,
Shattering my loneliness into glassy shards.

The epiphany haunts my dreams
Haunts my waking hours–
I live in perpetual calm
Like the Mona Lisa's eternal smile.

When I kiss her full, warm lips
 I feel God smiling over us–
When we embrace, I feel peace
Wrapping us in certain calm.

Her soft hands knead my back
Or stroke my waiting fingers
Caressing, soothing, whispering–
An understood touch.

We dance in concert to music
Played on a silent piano
The melody lilting, lifting,
A song only we hear.

The Marriage of Kindred Souls

The marriage of kindred souls, blessed by grace
Sacred union binding woman and man
An eternal coupling, a lasting embrace
Fulfilling nature's meaning, a plan.

Thus he and she become us and we, and
Encircle family and friend,
Their aura wrapped in ivy
They meld into one.

Marriage envelops and captures
Friend and foe in perpetual love
A miracle of love's rapture
The sum of one from diverse parts.

They share their joy, their peace
Forever young, forever bound.

The Fight Song of J Educagedin

Prologue:

If I thought my response
Would be to one who would dare
Change the almighty system,
I would take very great care
Not to let him be declared anathema
By thinking or acting on his own fare.

Let us go then you and I
Now that the sun has lightened the morning sky
To classroom buildings and lecture halls
And look and listen like open-mouthed fools;
Let us hear of names and dates and places
Of the hows and whys of social graces;
Let us learn how to scan a verse
So, we can judge which lines are worse.

Into the Union the students come and go
Talking of going to a movie show.

The white smoke that swirls from a teacher's pipe
The white smoke that's blown into a student's eyes
Rises to the ceiling lights
And curls around the fluorescent
And joins the general sleep.
And indeed, there will be time
For the white smoke that lies too deep
Scratching its back upon the ceiling;
There will be time, there will be time,
To prepare a pony for the tests you meet;
There will be time, there will be time

And time for all the works and ways of hands
That lift and drop an answer on your desk.
Time for you and time for me
And time for both of us to pass
In this and every other class
Before the taking of a bachelor's degree.

Into the Union the students come and go
Talking of going to a movie show.

And indeed, there will be time
To wonder, "Do I care?" and "Do I care?"
Time to turn around in my chair
And scratch my long blond hair
(They will say, "How he looks so fine,")
My tee shirt, stained with tiny specks of wine,
My Nikes blue and worn, but certainly in sync
Do I dare
Disturb the sleeping universe?

In a minute, there is time
For lectures and sermons that a thought will reverse
For I have heard them all already, heard them all,
Have heard them in evenings, mornings and afternoons;
I have measured out my life in lecture rooms,
I know the voices crying with a sighing call
Beneath the lecture in a farther room,
So how should I presume?
And I have known the legs already, known them all,
The legs that fix you in a formulated phase;
And when I am formulated, sprawling on the back seat,
When I am wriggling in a thrall,
Then how should I begin
To spit out the butt ends of days.
And how should I presume?
And I have known the arms already, known them all,
Arms that are braceleted, tattooed and bare

But in the sunlight, show a wear and tear.
Is it perfume from a dress
That makes my mind a mess?
Arms that lie along a dress or wrap about a boy.
And how should I presume

And how can I begin?

Shall I say, I have gone at dawn through narrow streets
And watched the smoke rise from pipes
Of deadly air from factories, blotting out the windows?
I should have been an Uber driver
Scuttling along deserted roads.

And the afternoon, the evening sleeps so peacefully
Smoothed by long, long dreams,
Asleep, asleep, or so it seems;
Stretched on the back seat, you and me
Should I, after the wine and pot mix,
Have the strength to reach a climax?
But though I have drunk and slept and dreamt
Though I have seen my head (locks and all) brought
In upon a pizza tray.
I am no priest-there is no time to pray.
And I have let it pass as the girl ate a snicker
And in short, I was ashamed.

And would it have been worth it after all
After the classes, the drive-in, the wine
Along the lover's lane, among some talk of yours and mine,
To have torn off her panties with a smile,
To have squeezed the two of us into a ball
And roll to some overwhelming passion,
To say "I am D H Lawrence come from the dead
Come back to tell you all–"
If she settling a car cushion under her head
Should say, "This is not the right time of the month at all.
This is not the time at all."
And would it have been worth it after all,
Would I have been worthwhile

After the movie, and the parking and the narrow street,
After the classes, after the booze, after the back seat
And this and so much more,
It is impossible to say just what I mean!
But as if somehow my nerves could scream,
Would it have been worthwhile
If she settling a cushion while pushing me away,
Turning her face should say,
"This is not the right time of the month at all!
This is not the time at all."

No, I am not Einstein nor was meant to be!
I'm a student, one that will do
To fill a class, ask a question or two,
Humor the prof, no doubt an easy tool,
Indifferent, glad to be unused
Apathetic and insignificant
Full of high spirits, but a bit obtuse,
At times indeed, almost conspicuous
Almost at times, the class fool.

I grow old–I grow old
I cannot wear my shirt sleeves rolled.
Shall I let my hair grow? Do I dare to eat pizza?
I shall wear a double-breasted suit and walk in the plaza.
I have heard the call girls calling "Hi Ya!"
I'll pretend they don't know me.

I have seen them tempting college boys
Stroking their wavy hair
As the wind blows through it.

We have lingered in the chambers of the schoolroom
With harlots in red and pink and green
Till the bell to end class wakes us and we drown.

Circadia

April opened raw last year
Wet and rainy, cold with icy
Windswept days, black and lonely night
The dregs of long Winter.

The robins, frozen to barren limbs
Naked and shaking, unnested,
Bringers of no Spring, no light, no songs
Cried aloud, like children locked out of home.

The hard land cracked the plow
And farmers cursed the rock ice ground
That neither took nor held seed,
A closed, unyielding virgin earth.

At night, the stars stayed at home,
Huddled, distant fires
Wrapped in clean well-lighted spaces
Beyond the waning moon, clouded and hiding.

But old Adam knew the cold would end,
Knew the sun would come again
To save the robins, thaw the land, open the clouds
For moon and starlight once more.

Others prayed and begged their gods
Repented and lit ten penny candles,
Kneeled and whispered and bowed down
Despairing and defeated before cold white altars.

But old Adam endured and waited,
Rocking upright, watching the East,
Alone, unafraid and calm as time
Beat out the course of things to come.

May's light lifted flowers and
Greened the hard-brown earth
For seeding, planting, impregnating earth
Womb-full of tomorrow's promise.

And robins laughed, sang, caroled
From blooming treetops and new fences
All the warm sunny day till dusk
When warm night breezes blew the sun to sleep.

Happy farmers lit pipes and gazed
Upward to starry candles hung
Gleaming and white on a black altar,
Higher than prayers ever go.

The earth was born anew,
Rich with hope, good-feeling
Work to do, rewards sacrifices
To make, children to spring to life.

But the chair rocked and rocked
Under stars the old man had known before,
Under moony whiteness that darkness
Would cover before morning.

He knew May's giddy breath of life
Would blow away, and heavy Summer,
Sweaty and dusty till harvest,
Would weigh on him, and he'd rock slower.

June burst blooming and fertile
Warm, wild with wedding bells and wine
Ringing fruition, marriage and love
Through time and field, loud with triumph.

The sky sat high, unclouded, wide
And sea blue by day; at night crystal stars
Sparkled beyond a pale bright moon
That bathed the growing crops ghostly white.

Sweat stained, blue shirted farmers
Backs bent to the soil, red-necked
Groping at crops with gnarled hands,
Felt the glory of work with reward.

And children splashed in cedar creeks,
Naked and laughing, wet, innocent,
To the sun and each other's eyes,
Primeval, beautiful and alive.

But the gaunt old man rocked alone,
Silent, unsweating, blowing smoke
Into soft halos, curls that fused
Quickly into the humid, June air.

The old man knew the heat would grow
Like the crops, and robust, hearty June
Would melt thaw and dissolve itself
Into the oven of hot, draining July.
Steaming, milk-white skied July
Burnt the soil into dusty submission;
The cruel sun shimmered with hellfire
So bright no eyes could watch it.

Dust clouds trailed the sweat-soaked farmer
Trudging through his fields praying for rain.
Listless robins perched in silence
On wilting, leaning, heavy limbs.

The cedar creeks ran shallow,
The children splashed no more. They sat
Half-naked under shade trees sweating,
Talking quietly in a sheltered circle.

Nighttime was airless, unsleeping,
Full of stars that sat remote and smug
Hanging aloft in a distant, cooler realm
Beyond the heavy sweat of men.

Old Adam knew the rain
Would come amid cracks of thunder
Storming away the drought,
Slaking the thirsty earth with saving water.
So, he sat alone and rocked
Nodding in the endless steady motion
Until his black, knowing eyes, closed
Waiting August's saving rain.

Black squawking crows swooped down
Attacking the dying August corn,
Unafraid of the dry straw scarecrow
That hung arms akimbo on a rotted cross.

Adam's son cursed the black-winged devils
Cursed his limp straw protector
Cursed August's alabaster fire,
Cursed the rain that would not come.

Dry, whitening stalks of corn,
Plunged deep into once fertile earth
Straining for water, straining hard
To find lifesaving drops of water.

The children made lemonade and sat
Under shade trees telling stories.
The robins sank into brittle nests.
They never sang at all.

Adam rocked slowly and waited
Shading his black eyes with his hand
A transparent figure, reedy but firm
Rocking in the sun, waiting for rain.

The open, dusty mouth of earth
Drank the cooling September rain
In long, wet draughts like a child
Suckling for life on mother's breast.
The farmer gave thanks, standing tall
On his porch, puffing on a new pipe,

Sure his crops would survive,
Sure of harvest, a just reward for his labor.

The robins lifted from their nests
Refreshed and ready for the trip South
To lands of sun and warmth
Away from snow and harsh Winter.

The children watched the creek fill
And savored the last cool plunges
Before school and books and harvest
Captured them in the work of Autumn.
And Adam rocked knowing his son
Was proud of his fruitful labor
His precious crops alive and full,
Safe in Baptismal rain.

October winds swept the tall trees
Shaking them naked in flurries
Of red and yellow, their brown limbs
Creaking tired with age.

The cool winds whipped the farmer
Burning his face apple red
As he loaded, sold or stored
The fruits of harvest
The children skipping home from school
Bypassed the once precious cedar creek,
Now too cold to please their young bodies,
Too cool to mean welcome and relief.

The robins turned their breasts South
And fled the afternoon of the year
Before the frosty night of Winter
Clasped its mantle over them.

The old woman had died at Harvest last year,
And Adam thought of her
As he watched the fading red sun
Drop and sink into the Far end of the earth.

November snow swirled in smoky gusts,
Powdering the sore navel of earth,
Stripped raw and barren of crops
By rough, pulling hands clawing at her womb.

Dark, angry clouds rumbled through the skies
In huge gray black columns like armies,
Thundering and bellowing the return of Winter
As Autumn cowed away, shrunken and stoop-shouldered.

The children and the farmer gathered together
Clasped hands and bowed their heads
In thanks for shelter and food and warmth.
 For they had been saved from starving in Winter.

And Adam sat alone by the red fire
Watching it eat the limbs of trees
In a steady, unyielding, relentless way
That left the wood no chance for survival.

High, white the moon brightened
December night into daylight,
Its icy vise choked the throat of day
Squeezing the sunlight out of it,
Leaving only steel grey, thick clouds.

The crisp peal of Christmas bells
Summoned the farmer to candlelit altars;
They marched Indian file in step,
Called to dance to the strings of a harp.

Beneath the snow, beneath the trudging feet,
Lay the inert, cold, sleeping earth,
Eyes closed, dead-blind to the ceremonies
Unaware of the bells and caroling in the night.

Only the tired, worn old man
Rocking alone before the fire
Wrapped in blankets and memories

Knew better than to answer the bell.
He knew the earth lay dormant
But alive, lay asleep but not dead,
He knew the earth would rise again,
Grow again, sprout again and again and again.

The deadly cold grip of January closed
Its icy vise around the throat of day
Squeezing the sunlight out of it,
Leaving thick clouds of sickening grey.

And the child, wracked with pain and fever,
Coughed as he lay drowning in phlegm,
Lungs gasping for air, breath
Until his candle light faded and sank.

And when they woke the earth from its sleep
To take another to rest beneath the snow
When they stood weeping and sobbing dumbfounded
That all was surely as God wanted

The knobby, clenched fist of angry Adam
Shook in defiance at the hidden sun,
Shook with rage at being mortal,
Shook with conviction that nothing was immortal.

Freezing, February iced the land
Twisting the wintry vise in one
Final turn that choked and held everything
Lifeless in a moment of dead, airless calm.

Starless black heavens, numb and void
Grassless brown land stony still,
Childless, gray people, alone and afraid;
Lifeless, only son, lost in death.

Only the rocking chair moved on
Like an ancient pendulum;

A motion inside a vacuum–
A force among the dead, a living.
The slow turn of Winter to sun,
Eased the wintry vise and unlocked sunlight;
The sun shone brightly in the face of earth
And woke the sleeping land to Spring.

The grass creeped out to meet the sun
In small, green patches, frail but alive.
The plow cracked the awakening earth
Furrowing deep into her waiting, willing womb.
And the child of another day
Lay newly seeded in his mother's womb.
To last until March is to live once more.
Adam knew he had survived and endured.

New Child

The crease of sunlight inched above the edge
Of a new morning horizon
The hint that all will be renewed
With the first breath of the child.

The anxious cry for mother's milk
Loud, demanding, a baleful whine
Trusting that the parent will heed
The clarion call to feed him.

The rising temperature of love
Warms the young father and mother
Like a campfire surrounded by kids
Seeking shelter from cold unknown.

Listen brave new world to the child
Who changed your universe forever;
Listen, watch, protect, love
For his birth makes us young.

The journey leads through strange woods
Tracking unknown paths, winding roads
Along streets running, turning, circling,
Through the garden maze of living.

Lift your chins to mark the course
To find the way to your new home
Rich with love and safety, fearless
In your devotion to your family.

Whistler's Song

*G*rand mom whispered as she read from her Bible, its slick pages trimmed in gold leaf. Lying with her back against the sofa under a bright lamp, she oozed peace from her round, cherub face and tiny brown eyes. Chocolate eyes. Soft yet piercing, all knowing. Her four-foot-ten body sunk into the couch. Her black heavy shoes hung over the side. She never took off her shoes. At least she had shed her apron.

I did not want to leave her to walk two houses to my home and my mother.

Who would leave love and wisdom for anarchy and disapproval?

"I am going home Grand mom. I carried the vacuum upstairs. When you are done, leave it upstairs. I'll take it down for you. Don't try taking it down. You could fall and get hurt."

"Thank you. I like a clean house."

"Hey a guy has to take care of his best friend, doesn't he?"

"I pray for you every night," she said.

"Thanks for dinner. The roast beef melted in my mouth."

"Tell your mother I will see her tomorrow after she comes home from work."

"Sure."

I sensed trouble. The phone had rung earlier. Grand mom answered it and shooed me away. Grand mom may have heard what I had heard about mom's affair with a married man. Her divorce had made her a target for men. Protecting her was a full-time job for this fifteen year-old.

I leaned down and kissed Grand mom's forehead, sweaty, moist from the late summer heat wave. Her thin hair lay matted against her hairline.

Grand pop sat in his favorite high back arm chair, its upholstery worn where his elbows sank into the arms. He looked calm, regal even, while smoking a stogie, perched in front of the television. He'd worked all day in an unairconditioned garment factory. As always, he had come in from work and eaten his ritual hot cherry pepper, drank a large glass of water and changed into a clean tee shirt. He deserved to be tired. After dinner, he'd beaten me again in pinochle, laughing with each winning trick, each winning hand. He laughed from his head to his toes, not in derision but in the joy of winning. His huge, carpenter hands waved at me.

"Good night Pop."

"Buono notte, Marco," he said smiling through soft blue eyes, a contrast to his Calabrian heritage.

"Stop letting him win. It goes to his head," said Grand mom.

"Hah. He has a steel trap mind for cards. He wins fair and square. But I am learning. Next time I will win."

Grand pop laughed. "No be so sure."

"Marco, don't forget to have my daughter Grace Marie call me."

"Done."

I left feeling her eyes and her love following me like a guardian angel shadowing her charge.

As I sat on the concrete front steps of my home, the setting sun cast the row houses on both sides of the narrow block in shadows. The street crackled with the laughter of my black friends, Billy Boy, Jo Jo, and Sister Tish across the street. Billy Boy was tall, reedy and usually drunk. Jo Jo was a wiry dude, dangerous as the switch blade in his jeans. Tish flashed me a toothy smile. Her halter top bulged with fine brown pear shaped breasts. I'd tasted them more than once.

My white buddies, Choo Choo, Frank, and Reds threw a white pimple ball toward the telephone wires trying to hit them to score a hit in wire ball. Frank could spot a fly from a hundred feet at midnight. Choo could not catch a ball with a basket. Reds and I had more than one tussle over his sister Junie. The girl liked me from head to foot. Who says Catholic girls wait for marriage to get laid?

I turned on my transistor radio to Bobby Darin's, "Mack the Knife."

Bobby D was the essence of "cool," the void in the soul of Rock and Roll torn asunder by the death of Buddy Holly. James Dean was dead for four years. I was fifteen and felt alone in a hostile universe. I needed a drink.

Mom called from the open front porch window. "Marco. Are you going to work tomorrow?"

Interpretation: she needed money. I turned to look at her. She looked tired beyond her thirty-six years.

"I am cutting lawns."

She swigged her high ball, twirling the ice in the water glass. Her thin hands shook from her arthritis, her veins bulging across the back of her hands. She'd scalded her skin off her hands in a freak accident washing dishes in the kitchen sink after one of her parties with her friends.

"Grand mom wants you to call her tomorrow. She seemed worried about you."

Mom shrugged but her downcast eyes belied her nonchalance.

"My Mother worries about everyone."

"She looked upset like somebody gave her bad news. Wonder what that could be?"

Mom winced as if I'd slapped her hard. She feared Grand mom because Grand mom knew her, understood her and saw through Mom's self-serving lies.

"Okay," she said turning back to her television. She turned on her small black and white Emerson. She'd bought it from Billy Boy for five bucks, no questions asked.

Mom was not much taller than her mother. She had Grand pop's light blue eyes under light brown, almost blond hair. She was pretty in a down to earth way. She worked out every day doing calisthenics–to take off the fat from her hips and waist–and she could dance. She always bragged how she cleared the dance floor a thousand times jitter bugging to Glenn Miller. More than once she cut school to see Harry James. Rules were for other people. She danced to her rhythm, her beat.

I Love Lucy came on, so Mom would be duly amused for half an hour. I slipped inside and tiptoed up the creaky, wooden steps. I flopped on the bed and closed my tired eyes. I needed new glasses but they cost money and we had no money except for the dollar and a half in quarters in my jeans. I would have sold my twenty-two rifle but the most I could get was five bucks from Jo Jo. The loaded rifle was my insurance against intruders. Once a week I cleaned it while sitting on the front steps. The neighbors saw it and knew I was sending a message, meaning "Do not fuck with me or mine."

I nicknamed the gun "Holmes," an old street name.

The sun sank. I was glad for the darkness. It was like a new world had come to cover the world of hot light and desperate people groveling to stay alive.

I lay listening to the doo wop tunes from the Platters and Jackie

Wilson and Sam Cooke and the Drifters and the Del Vikings and the Five Satins crooning "In the still of the night," my favorite. I always made the guys stand with their hands over their chests when Freddy Paris sang the so-called national anthem of doo wop.

My self-composed whistling tune welled up in me and slipped from my lips in a low but throbbing whistle. It had come to me one night on one of my solitary nocturnal walks after curfew. It had no lyrics. It was a solo that poured out of my loneliness and defiance of the hollow feeling of being alone in a strange land.

Keats wrote, "Heard melodies are sweet but those unheard are sweeter; therefore, ye soft pipes, play on."

Whatever he meant, I think I too had an unheard melody. It is my song and I will keep it secret forever.

Mom's laughter cracked the silence. She had a throw-back your head, hearty laugh, infectious, genuine like a child surprised by a new bike at Christmas. I smiled admitting that I loved her though with her I could do nothing right. I felt good, almost happy like before my father left us. The days at Atlantic City beach under a sweltering sun or splashing in the surf, my thin body caught up in their arms as they raised me above the waves. I laughed as a child should laugh with his parents, a trusting carefree laugh, an assertion that the world was good, I was good. The best of times.

Then as if god wanted to punish me came the images that haunted me each night. The images of my mother naked in a man's arms. The man was older with black eyes and a salt and pepper mustache, a leering, smug man who sneered at me as I watched him plow into her while I stood mute and immobilized, transfixed in shame and horror and my mother moaning his name. "Jimmy, Jimmy, Jimmy."

I needed to get away.

I yelled down to my mother. "I am going to bed Mom. Don't wake me."

"Good night Marco. Sweet dreams. Hope you make good money tomorrow."

It was after ten when I climbed out of the rear window and shimmied down the gas stand pipe to the alley behind the house. I walked quickly to the street and headed away from the guys playing wire ball. I did not want their company nor did I want a quick bang from "Tish the Dish." I wanted to walk free and alone. I wanted to feel clean.

I walked down Walton Street, past nicer homes with porches

and lawns and people sitting in their living rooms watching TV. I headed into Fairmount Park near Valley Green. The Wissahickon Creek cut through the dark woods, a liquid snake winding along a crooked path to the Schuykill River and the heart of the City.

The woods crackled with the mating call of crickets lusting in heat of Summer. Hard to imagine two crickets screwing. WIBG radio played the best doo wop songs. I was walking in step with the smooth voice of Tony Williams and the dynamic energy of Jackie Wilson and the Diamonds and the Jive Five and the Rivieras and the Marcels. I had my own world for at least a few hours. The full moon hung above me like a street lamp from God. Grand mom believed in God. I believed in her.

Tired, I trudged home, careful to avoid the Cops, especially Conway, a beer-bellied bully who liked to crack people with his night stick. A squad car raced behind me, its lights flashing.

"Stop D'Amato. You are past curfew."

Conway.

I started to run. But I tripped on a cracked sidewalk landing face first. The bastard smashed his billy club across the back of my head. Stunned, I lay there as he pummeled my arms and legs. He reeked of cheap whiskey as he knelt next to me and whispered in his best Irish accent.

"Marco, me Lad. You are one dumb dago boy. I'll let ye go and please send your lovely mama Gracie my best regards. Now limp your lame ass home before I run ye in."

The mention of mom hurt more than the billy club.

If I could get away with it, I'd shoot his nuts off.

I limped my way home, cringing in pain and embarrassment with every step. Smith Street was empty. Grand mom's house was dark. There was a light in my front window. Mom always left one on so any robbers would think we were awake and would bypass us. Hell, they bypassed us because we had nothing worth stealing. Instead of reclimbing the stand pipe to my bedroom, I crawled through the front window past mom snoring, curled up in her chair like a child waiting for her mother to tuck her in. Her TV was still on. Her drinking glass laid empty on the coffee table.

I crept up the stairs to my room feeling like a whipped dog. I crawled into bed, resting against a pillow and the barrel of my rifle. I turned on the radio to Bobby Darin's "Dream Lover." Tears welled up as my back, legs, and shoulders throbbed in pain, but I held them back. Conway would not get away with this. Someday I would square up with him.

"Nobody makes me cry."

I dozed off until I heard the downstairs phone ring. Mom answered and spoke so low I could not hear her. She laughed a coy, giggling laugh she used around men. I lay awake waiting and hoping that I was waiting in vain.

Five minutes passed with no knock on the front door. Ten minutes passed. All was quiet. I needed to sleep but my heart could have outraced the field at the Kentucky Derby. The adrenalin eased the pain. I was wide awake. If he showed up, I'd kill the bastard and claim self-defense.

Tap, tap, tap on the front door. He was here. Mom opened the door.

"Hi Hon. Come in before Marco hears anything. Hurry."

I took a deep breath and grabbed the rifle. I double checked to make sure it was not loaded. I had enough abuse for one night. Time to fight back.

I eased down the steps toward the living room. I wheeled in, my gun at the ready. Empty.

Dim light filled the doorway to her bedroom. I edged along the corridor to the muffled sounds of two people struggling to shed their clothes. Mom lay naked on the bed, her arms extended to Jimmy. His ass mooned me as he climbed on top of her. Nausea mixed with fear, hurt, self-loathing in a suffocating emotional cocktail.

Her arms wrapped around his neck. Her fingers raced through his jet-black hair, slicked with oil or brill cream.

"Yes, my Jimmy," she said.

I rushed behind Jimmy and pressed the rifle barrel to the back of his head. "Get off her or you are a dead chump in the truest sense of the word," I said.

Jimmy's back arched as if a bolt of electricity had shot up his ass.

"What the fuck?" he said.

Mom pushed away from Jimmy, covering her breasts. "Marco. O my god. Put the gun down. Now. Are you crazy!?"

"You bet I am. Get up, Jimmy."

"Hey kid. Put away the gun," said Jimmy with palpable fear in his voice.

"I am going to shoot you Jimmy. You see, I burst in on a man raping my mother. I thought it was the Mount Airy rapist. The cops will like that story. It solves a lot of open cases."

"No, no kid. I will go. Just let me get dressed."

"I'd rather shoot you. It is the only way to chase away the images in my head. Yes. I will kill you. Say a last prayer."

Mom pulled on her night gown. She was pale, her eyes wide as Broad Street.

"Marco. Stop it now. Please Marco. I am your mother. I want you to put down the gun."

I tapped the barrel of the gun on Jimmy's head. "No mother dearest. I want to kill him if only to make you suffer."

"Marco. No, No, No." said mother Grace.

My hands shook but I could not miss the shot. One bullet and the nightmare ends.

"Put it down, my boy," said Grand mom from behind.

Startled I wheeled my head around. "Grand mom."

"Hand me the gun. What the mother does is on the soul of the mother. Your sin would be to ruin your life because of her sins."

I backed out of the room. Grand mom took the gun.

"You two get dressed. The boyfriend here, goes, and vows to never return. Grace, you go take a shower like it is a Baptism, so God can forgive you."

Jimmy pulled on his pants sans underwear and left like he had a hot pepper up his butt.

Grand mom ran her hand across my face, my forehead and pulled my head to her breast.

"Go back to your bed, Marco. Come for dinner tomorrow night. I need to talk to my daughter. Go with God, mio nipote."

I hugged her. "Yes. I will do as you say." The next thing I heard was a slap and my mother's yelp.

"Putana in sangue," said Grand mom.

Whore in the blood.

*M*y tee shirt clung to my chest and back like an extra layer of skin. After cutting six lawns, I had four dollars and fifty cents. I had two more jobs lined up but lack of sleep and the hundred-degree humidity had sapped my strength. I washed my hands with a spigot in the back yard. I slapped water down my head and shoulders. My body ached from head to toe. Screw Jimmy. I should have shot that prick Conway.

I'd keep the money from Mom. I'd take Junie to see the new Elvis movie, "King Creole." Maybe we'd share ice cream, too, and whatever else she wanted to do.

I walked slowly up Smith Street. Three-story brick homes lined the treeless, narrow street, capturing the heat like two sides of a pizza oven. Nothing moved. I passed Grand mom's house and heard the whirr of the vacuum cleaner from the front bedroom on the second story. If she followed her routine, she'd be done in about fifteen minutes. I needed to carry that vacuum down the steps for her and I needed to talk to her. She had saved me from myself. I would have shot Jimmy. I would have committed suicide by going to jail. How she showed up at that hour, only she and God knew. I had enough money to get her a new rosary.

I hurried upstairs to my room, stripped and headed to the shower. The warm water soothed my aches, relaxed my muscles. Renewed, I dressed in clean jeans and headed to Grand mom's. I opened her front door just as she came crashing down the wooden stairs. Her body tumbled and twisted the fifteen steps to the bottom followed by the vacuum cleaner that landed against the side of her head. She lay in a heap. Her eyes rolled back in her head. But she did not pass out.

"Help me," she said.

I stood stock still trying to figure out what to do. I was afraid to move her, but I lifted the vacuum from her body and hurled it across the room.

"Grand mom. Why didn't you wait for me? What shall I do?"

"Call."

I raced to the phone and called the operator. The ambulance would be ten minutes.

Grand mom moaned in pain. "It hurts. O God it hurts," she said. "Mea culpa mio Dio!"

She started choking, her round cheeks puffed out gasping for air. There was no blood, but she had turned milk white like a doll.

I tried to lift her, but she cried out in pain. One of her ribs was sticking out through her skin on her left side. I felt helpless and guilty. If only I had come one minute sooner. She had saved me, and I had failed her.

"Marco. Forgive your mother. She is only human. Remember she is a woman first and your mother second. Forgive her for her sins and you will save yourself."

"You waited for me to come home. That phone call you got warned you about Jimmy. His wife called you, didn't she? You are hurt for protecting me and my mother."

"Only you, my Son."

Her head went limp at the neck. A choking gurgle shook her whole body until she went limp, and then silent. She was gone. I pounded both fists on the stairs and let out a primeval scream.

"Noooooooooo!!"

*A*fter the funeral director had taken Grand mom, Mom and I sat across from each other at our metal kitchen table. She had trash picked the table from a house in Chestnut Hill. Billy Boy gave us the non-matching wooden chairs. The ceiling was a drop ceiling just over six feet high. A Pullman kitchen without the train.

A small window looked out on the back alley. We had a prime view of trash cans and hungry rats.

The breakfast dishes laid stacked in the sink, stained yellow with touches of dried egg and bacon and scraps of toast. The sink was cracked on both sides. A water bug breeding ground.

The black, greasy frying pan lay on the stove top. I'd need a Brillo pad to scrub it. Doing the dishes was my chore. Mom was afraid of getting scalded again. Great excuse, but I did not mind her using me a little.

Mom's eyes were redder than tomato sauce. Her hair was tied up in a bun. She looked young, pretty, and forlorn.

Mom poured each of us a glass of Grand pop's homemade wine. She filled the water glasses to near the top. Guzzling that much dago red wine at once would cripple Superman.

"To my Mom," she said clicking our glasses.

"Yes. To Grand mom. Sempre." She looked nothing like Grand mom.

Mom smacked her lips, now wet and red with wine. Reminded me of Grand pop at dinner, washing down his supper.

"Your Grandfather will follow her soon. They were so close."

"I won't let him die. I will stay close to him."

"Me too," she said. "I wonder if she told him about Jimmy? I hope not. Christmas. He'd slap me silly."

"If he knew about Jimmy he would have taken a strap to you. I won't tell him. Your exploits are safe with me, and Grand mom would have been too proud to tell anybody. If he hears anything, it will be from the gossips in the neighborhood."

I wanted to smack her myself but she needed protection, not a whack across her face.

Mom's lips quivered, "I cannot believe, she is gone. She hated me. My own mother hated me. She called me a whore. I am so sorry. God help me. I am so ashamed."

I clutched her bony hand. "No, Mother. No one loved you more than Grand mom. She told me so at the end. You disappointed her but nothing could ever make her hate you. Or me."

Mom squeezed my hand, hard, as if to hold me in her vise. She needed me. "I am so sorry, Marco, for everything. I will get rid of Jimmy. I will be a better mother. I owe that much to you and my Mother. Will you forgive me?"

"Yes mother. We both need forgiveness, don't we?"

"I guess so. I just want a normal life. Your father ruined that. Am I so hard to love?"

"You are too easy to love, Dear Mother."

Her face screwed up into a mask of hurt and shame.

"I am not a whore."

"We are all sinners, Mom."

"Would you have killed Jimmy?"

"Probably. It is so easy for anyone to kill another human being isn't it? Holmes would have served his purpose."

She leaned close and whispered as if god was listening. "Would you have killed me too?"

My heart jumped for the truth was that I probably would have killed her too and then myself.

"No. Mom."

"You are all I have, Marco."

Tell that to Jimmy.

"Mom, we are separate people. You are you and I am me. The parental relationship is sacred but so is our identity. I am me and you are you as individuals. Grand mom made me see that we owe each other nothing we do not want to give freely. I love you for who you are. Do you understand what I am saying?"

Mom took a long swig of wine. "I think so. I must call Jimmy. I must tell him good bye. I have to."

"Thanks Mom but do not do it on my account. Live your own life and I will live mine. Fair enough?"

"Yes. I see your point. I see everything so clearly now. I will send him away for my sake, not yours."

"Good move."

"I love you Marco."

"Thank you, Mother. Now learn to love yourself."

"That is what Grand mom always said. Love yourself enough to do right. I gotta call Jimmy. He will be very upset. He really is a good guy."

"Sure."

Jimmy would never go away. He'd just reappear with a different name and a different hairy ass.

I finished the wine in silence.

I cleaned the dishes and frying pan using a sponge and wiped them clean. I washed out my wine glass. I was done drinking for now. I had something to do.

I walked out the front door to the middle of the street carrying Holmes. I found the rifle behind Grand mom's washing machine.

The night air was brutally still, holding the street in a heavy mantle of heat and humidity.

The second-floor windows reflected along the street like so many ghosts witnessing a funeral.

The neighbors were gathered in small circles, gabbing and pointing at our house. The crowd turned silent as I strode down the street, my head up, my back straight like a Marine on parade.

"Bad Ass Marco gonna shoot somebody," said Billy Boy. "I want to see this."

"Won't be me," said Tish. "I put sugar in his coffee."

"Marco, who's gonna die for your Grand mom dying?" asked Billy Boy. "Somebody gotta pay the price."

How do you shoot god?

Tish called out. "That man is a born killer. Born and raised. I know that for a fact. Look at them eyes. Step back you fools and let the man pass or face his wrath, praise Jesus."

Tonight, I had seen life as I had never seen it before. I'd matured ten years in one minute.

I walked to the sewer at the end of the block. I held up the rifle to the crowd.

"Hey, this fucking gun is not who I am!"

I fired a one-shot salute into the air. I placed the rifle on the ground and kicked it down the sewer. "Good bye, Holmes."

"Damn," said Billy Boy.

"Praise Jesus," said Tish. "I thought he was a killer and one us be dead. He ain't no such thing."

"He is a man, a real man," said Billy Boy.

My tune came to me as I walked away from Smith Street whistling my song aloud, the ballad of my life ringing in harmony with my soul.

I shall whistle it forever.

Roland at the Pass

The Montagnard people of Vietnam are indigenous to the Central Highlands area surrounding the City of Pleiku. They are courageous fighters, independent, and speak Bru, a chain dialect Khmer -Mon spoken in Laos and Thailand. To them the Vietnam War was a war of liberation, and to them Ho Chi Minh was a destroyer not a unifier, so they eagerly joined forces with the American Army to fight the North Vietnamese Army.

When Special Forces Captain Roland Valente accepted the assignment to lead the Montagnard fighters against the North Vietnamese, he welcomed the rare assignment, so he could use his enhanced language skills. Now he was ready to go home. The war was lost, and he and his aide, Sergeant Joseph Michael Kelly, planned to live another day.

A hard tap on his shoulder from Thanh, the Montagnard leader spun him around.

"We have a problem, Captain," said Thanh. The hot sun framed Thanh's short, wiry body, cast iron strong under black pajamas down to his worn balata shoes.

Thanh's pencil thin mustache bent downward in a scowl.

"What problem?"

Thanh tugged on his shirt. "Come. I will show you."

I motioned Kelly to join us. He rolled his Irish blue eyes and followed.

Roland was a foot taller than Thanh and ten years younger, but Thanh could fight with the ferocity and cunning of any Special Forces Soldier.

Roland followed him along the rim of the Marble mountains to a vantage point above the valley near Pleiku. Two days ago, the four thousand American troops stationed there had crept away to a makeshift airfield, leaving behind the Montagnards, and many of them women and children. Roland slapped at the mosquitos and tiny black flies nipping at his neck. In two days, the only one nipping on his neck would be his wife Margarete. "Soon Baby, soon."

Thanh pointed to the northeast. "There. You can see the yellow jeep of Giao Vinh. He has at least one hundred men with him. He is heading toward the encampment. He will take revenge on the people for the victories we won and the marijuana field we burned. My men cannot get there in time. What shall we do?"

"The smoke from that fire kept me high for a week," said Kelly.

I wanted to go home. So too did Kelly. A delay may cause us to miss the chopper due to take us away in one hour.

"Okay here is what we can do. Kelly and I will ambush the jeep. If we can kill Giao Vinh, we can all get away. You get your people out of the encampment and get away."

Thanh nodded. "That is a good plan. But do not get your ass shot off."

"Captain. We cannot hold out against those odds. Let's call the chopper, get it here sooner and boogie out of here," said Kelly.

"Our mission is over when those people are safe. Thanh, get moving. Kelly, follow me and that is an order to each of you."

"Captain, this is madness. If Giao Vinh goes for the encampment, that means he will not get near us and we can skate out of here. Let's think of ourselves and not throw our lives away."

"You have your orders," said Roland.

Thanh saluted and turned away headed for the encampment.

Kelly's face reddened, as his eyes squinted in shear anger. "I swear, I will kill both of us before I let them take us alive."

We sped down the mountain toward a ledge overlooking the dirt road. There were at least one hundred and eighty of Giao Vinh's men headed towards us. They were smoking joints and laughing. The victors.

"When the Jeep gets in range, fire," said Roland.

"Okay."

I will go over there so we have a two-man cross fire. Aim for the jeep tires. We will force Giao Vinh into the open and finish him off. Then we high tail it to the landing zone."

"Got it."

A minute later Roland and Kelly opened fire on the jeep. The bullets blew out the windshield and caught one of the tires. Giao Vinh cursed aloud as his men took cover. Roland kept firing at the Jeep.

Giao emerged and Roland opened fire on him. A bullet nicked Giao Vinh's arm sending him down, but the jeep shielded him from the crossfire. Giao Vinh shouted to his men to fan out and find the snipers.

Roland knew he had missed killing Giao Vinh, but he had taken his attention away from the encampment.

Mission accomplished.

"Kelly. Let's roll," he said.

The two soldiers scampered across the face of the mountain and sped towards the landing zone.

Each step was one step closer to his wife Margarete, his home.

They reached the landing zone having taken no fire. Had Giao Vinh returned his attention to the Montagnards?

The whirr of the helicopter from the southwest meant a trip home was at hand. The chopper was flying high but began its descent into the flattened grass of the meadow. The two soldiers rushed from cover, smiling, shouting, their arms waving.

The chopper stopped two hundred yards away, a mere sprint to safety. Then the crash of exploding mortar shells hit the site. Roland's life flooded before him. Giao Vinh had pursued them and had waited for them to lead him to the chopper, one last prize of war.

A shell crashed into the chopper and exploded the copter; Kelly screamed, "Nooooo!!!"

From two sides Giao Vinh's men emerged, calling for the Americans to surrender.

"They want us to surrender," said Roland.

Kelly shook his head, "Never. He opened his mouth to the gun barrel and fired. His brain matter splattered through the air, shreds landing on Roland. Roland sank to his knees, his body numb, his mind in a funk.

"Drop your weapon," said Giao Vinh walking towards him, smiling like Satan at the gates of Hell.

The sound of his voice roused Roland. His father always said, "Evil is made possible by good men who do nothing to stop it."

He had stopped Giao Vinh. He had sacrificed as Christ had sacrificed and proved the value of his teachings.

"Good bye Margarete," he whispered.

The enemy was closing in. The stench of marijuana sifted through the hot air. The flames from the fiery chopper roared in his face, singeing his cheeks and neck. He was in hell.

Roland quickly turned his rifle on Giao Vinh and fired, killing him instantly. A sweet sense of happiness engulfed him before the hail of bullets killed him.

From the top of the Marble Mountains, Thanh saluted him and made the sign of the cross, though he was a devout Sadi Aminist. Tonight, he would sit safely around a low fire and play a tune on his flute to a brave man from another religion.

Savanna at Four

She is four but cannot talk.
She is four but cannot walk.
She is four her eyes alight.
She is four her smile so bright.

Her doctors say no, nay, never
Will she walk or talk ever.
They do not see her heart,
They do not know her heart.

Her spirit is cast in steely love
Iron will, velvet glove.
Her innocence shining clear,
Her body struggles, sans fear.

Many cherish this girl,
Praying, tearing, all awhirl.
Yet she soothes their fears
Turning sadness to cheers.

Do they not see God's grace
Beaming from her face?
Hear her sweet voice,
Trying to call out, rejoice,
Full of life so precious
Full of the life inside us?

She is four and blest
She is four, share her quest.
She is four enriching All
She is four standing Tall.

Sunset Love

The eternal December mantle
Covers my cloudy gaze.
I shall sleep in her heart and arms
For timeless, unending days.

Her smile, wit and charm
Softens cold, cruel death.
I do not fear the looming dark
The imminent last breath.

No. I savor the moment
Relish the final glimmer of light
Rejoice in feeling needed, loved,
Fulfilled beyond sound and sight.

To die in love is to prevail
To prevail is to perpetually endure.
To endure is to win in the after life
In heaven, immortal, secure.

To Van Gogh

The sunflowers glow from a porcelain vase
Wind thrashes the starry, starry sky.
Angry crows attack the wheat field
Recoiling from the harsh force of nature.

Oceans of emotion in one brush stroke
So much humanity in potatoes
The pain in a ghostly self portrait
Like painting yourself as a joke.

Is not your struggling soul
The essence of your art?
Your images torture me, routing
The turmoil in my heart and mind.

You rush hot blood through my veins,
A devilish surge of mocking pain,
A flash flood drowning my senses
A truth I feel more than see.

Last Rites

Daily the past courses my mind
Choices I made from love or fear
Decisions squeezed by the need for money
Moments when I lacked the courage to act.

Listening to an old record or tape
Scenes of triumph and cowardice
The forked road of my journey
Lunging ahead, falling back.

Now is the time for Endgame
Still writing, thinking, dreaming
Not caring who will care if I die,
But confident I LIVED my life

Neither in futility nor bravado
Stood up for myself, my friends,
My family, my beliefs, my work.
I've lived, and not simply survived.

Ro Ro Morse,
Philly's Most Unusual Detective

Story One: Murder in the Tavern

Chapter One

*P*hiladelphia Homicide Detective Rowena Morse twirled her shoulder length frosted blond hair end around her right forefinger. She smiled her best flirt as Al, the bar owner, filled her cocktail glass with a fresh margarita, her favorite Summertime cocktail.

"On me, Miss Detective Ro Ro."

Al stood six-four, a foot taller than Ro, and weighed twice her hundred and forty-one pounds. Al was her contemporary at fifty-two years-old, though Ro looked a dozen years younger thanks to a daily regimen of a twenty-minute workout on her Chuck Norris home gym.

"Thanks Al. You are the Best."

Al had spent ten plus years trying to get her in bed, all in vain. She was a lifetime widow and had made one mistake falling in love with a tall. handsome man with a sly smile and the moral fiber of a worm. Plus, Al was married rendering him anathema.

The five PM happy hour bell rang. In five minutes, O'Grady's bar would be two deep with a raucous crowd from the Mount Airy neighborhood. On cue, the locals poured in scrambling for precious empty bar stools preferably near a TV. Ro Ro knew all of them and their families going back to her grammar school days at Holy Cross. The chatter at the bar ranged from arguments about Trump to the Philadelphia Eagles, Flyers, Sixers, and Phillies. Ro had zero interest in sports, despised Trump, Hypocrite Hillary, Mayor Kenney, and both Houses of Congress.

She swirled a stir straw around her glass saying hello to the same people who she'd grown bored with but treasured. The gang were mainly Kool Aid drinking Catholics who considered original thought an off shoot of original sin. They were endearing knuckle heads. Hearts of gold. Heads of lead.

She was the only female in the bar, but no man here dared to challenge her presence.

A new face appeared in the doorway. Dark eyes, jet black hair, and a scowl running jaw to jaw across his square face. Dressed in a full-length brown leather coat, a crimson turtleneck, and jeans, he crossed the room in three long strides, his leather boot heels echoing his presence, and settled into a corner booth. The slight bulge under the coat meant he was carrying, probably a thirty-eight.

A minute later, the front door opened to Jimmy the Jumper Roscoe, local bookie, card cheat, and renowned wielder of a switch blade. His gray fedora hung tightly along his orange red hair line. He nodded to Al, swung his hand in a circle, a signal to buy the house. The grateful fools thanked Jumper for buying them drinks with money they had lost to him on numbers, football bets, and short-term loans with enough vig to drown a whale. Jumper shook hands with the crowd before settling into the booth with the stranger. They did not shake hands.

Her memory light turned on. The stranger was Germantown John Mancuso. G Town John was his street name. Local legend had it that G Town John was the toughest street fighter in Philly. Her dead ex-husband grew up with G Town John.

Jumper meeting G Town in person meant he was sending someone here a message.

Normally she left by five-thirty, but lounging at home alone was far less interesting than watching the two thugs in the booth from the mirror over the bar. Bottles of Tullamore Dew, Red Breast, John Powers, and Paddy's lined the back bar. The Irish angels, Al called them, for they made men sing "Danny Boy" and "Whiskey in the Jar" like they were solemn hymns.

Joey the Moocher McKee sidled his lithe, sixty-year-old carcass toward the corner booth. Joey had not won a bet in decades, so it would not surprise Ro Ro if Joey was in debt over the top of his shock of gray hair. Joey walked to the table smiling, but the smile melted away like snow awash in a rain storm. Joey turned a whiter shade of pale as G Town John patted his chest bulge.

Al walked from behind the bar, motioning for the crowd to follow him. Twenty men surrounded Joey.

Al pointed to Jumper. "Leave Joey alone. He's got pancreatic cancer. Whatever he owes we will cover it when he passes. And any bets you take from him from here on out are on you."

The crowd murmured their support. Then Tony, little boss De Giacomo, walked in front of Al. Little Tony was a cousin of Al's and a worse loser than Joey. His pencil mustache and squinty eyes created the distinct impression of a weasel in a black pea coat, sneaky and out of season. He wore high top sneakers that squeaked with each step he took. Tony had the smallest feet on record. The high tops were probably a kid's size ten. Growing up, Tony's pint size shoes earned him nicknames like Wussy Foot, Mini Guinea, and Rapid Rabbit. Ro suspected he was showing up to deflect Jumper to focus on Joey. He creeped her out.

G Town pulled his gun and yanked Joey by his shirt collar across the table.

"Don't mess with us, punk," said G Town.

Joey cried out, "No John G. I'll get the dough. I swear on my mother's eyes."

"Your mother is as dead as you will be if you don't pay us," said Jumper.

Ro swung off her stool, her thirty-eight in hand and cocked it, pointing the barrel at G Town.

"Go back to Germantown. Now!"

The bar turned deadly quiet. For a long moment no one moved. You could hear a fly burp.

"Who's the chick?" asked G Town.

Al's lips curled in a snickering smile. "Mount Airy's finest cop. Screw with her and she'll spread your brains across the wall."

G Town slid the gun back into his holster. "This ain't over," he said.

"That's right," said Jumper.

"Get out and don't ever come back," said Al.

G Town stopped at the doorway. "There are dead beats here who owe us. We will collect. As for you Miss Nice Body, don't ever pull a gun on me again or maybe you will get one of your boobs shot off."

Rowena glared laser beams at him. Her heart raced like Smarty Jones down the stretch. "Go for it anytime you grease ball."

"Wait I remember you. You married Ricky Rawlings. Yeah. You were Ricky's broad. You are looking hot Mrs. Rawlings," said Germantown.

"The name is Detective Morse."

"Yeah. A real hard head. That's what Ricky told me. Too bad about Ricky and the car accident. I miss the man. Do you?"

"If you miss him then just go to hell. His lying, cheating ass is there waiting for you."

"Touche Nice Boobs. Ricky was small potatoes next to you." G Town John blew her a kiss and walked out.

The bar erupted in cheers. Al hugged her, a little too closely.

"Drinks on the house," said Al.

The men gathered around her singing, "For she's a jolly good fellow."

"What a chorus of knuckle heads," she said. The praise warmed her like brandy pouring down her insides.

An hour later, her hand on her gun, Ro walked three blocks to her twin stone and stucco home on East Mount Airy Avenue. The tree-lined street held enough ambush opportunities to scare Super Woman.

She showered to get her body relaxed, her mind calmed. She admitted to herself that she wanted to shoot Germantown John just like she wanted to shoot her dead husband Ricky when she caught him cheating on her with Julie Monaco, a skank from Germantown. Julie Monaco had a link to G Town John, What was it?

At eleven thirty, she crawled into bed, feeling happy that she had stood up for Joey and backed down Germantown John. Her parents were dead, so she had no one with whom to share her pride. They had never encouraged her. They bullied her as surely as Germantown John had bullied Joey. Her mother would dine on steak while taunting her with, "Hot dogs for you," and she would say this while holding a forkful of prime rib. And her father never said a word in her defense. College was out of the question despite her record of straight As. "Girls don't need college. They need a good husband and lots of kids to keep him home," said her mother at least eighty thousand times.

She'd left their home at twenty, escaping like a lamb running from hungry wolves. For six months she lived at the YWCA on Chestnut Street in Center City, that was until she took a police exam and aced it. She was a survivor. Satisfied with her fate, she closed her eyes and slept soundly until her cell phone blared at six thirty. The caller ID read "Malone."

Her affair with Bart had ended months ago. He must be drunk

to call her.

Anxious, she pushed the green button on her iPhone.

"This is Detective Morse."

"Ro Ro. It's Bart Malone. I just found Al O'Grady shot dead in his bar. You better get over here."

Ro gasped, "What? Are you pulling my leg?"

"I am not that nuts. I called it in. CSU is on the way. The case will more than likely go to you, so get your sweet buns over here, pronto."

"Secure the scene."

"Done."

She raced to the bathroom for a quick pee. She splashed water across her face. Her wrinkles were showing. No time for make-up. No time to shower. She plied her body with a bath gel and soft sponge. She rinsed her teeth with a mouthful of Listerine and glanced at the mirror. She winced at the reflection of a baggy-eyed woman who looked older than thirty-six. She dressed in a dark gray pants suit, in need of pressing, and a black silk blouse. She strapped on her double-sided holster. The right side held her thirty-eight caliber service revolver. The left side held a twenty-two caliber pistol, a gift from her ex-husband. She was an expert with both hands. Rowena fled the house, jogging in flat shoes towards O'Grady's, anxious to get after whoever shot Al and curious as to why Bart called her directly.

All the way to O'Grady's her mind swirled around one question. Had she gotten Aloysius Francis O'Grady murdered by antagonizing Germantown John? Dagos don't like women who make them look bad. Al stood up to the thug, too. And what was Bart Malone doing in O'Grady's so early?

She crossed the bumpy cobblestones on Germantown Avenue, barely grasping the inescapable fact that Al O'Grady was dead, part of Mount Airy was dead. Somebody was going to pay.

Rowena knelt beside Al's body supine on the ceramic tile floor next to the bar. His bloody shirt clung to him. A red badge of courage, she thought.

"I covered his face with a table cloth after I closed his eyes," said Malone.

Rowena avoided looking at Bart, a.k.a Black Bart, named after the Old Western bandit who robbed Wells Fargo stage coaches in California. Malone was a thief in his own right but a good-looking one.

She edged the tablecloth away from Al's face, fearful he would somehow see her and cast guilt on her. He'd been shot in the chest twice at close range. Upturned bar stools were set in a neat row along the bar, meaning he'd done a post-close cleanup, so the murder had taken place sometime after two AM. Al would have locked the door, so he must have let the killer inside. The killer was somebody Al knew and trusted. Somebody she probably knew as well. One of the stools was slightly put out of line to the right. Al was an ex-Marine and never let anything get out of order.

The CSU team arrived, headed by Dr. Charles "Docky" Poteet, a product of Sharpnack Street in lower Mount Airy. Docky played linebacker at Germantown High and at Temple. He had street smarts from his Dreadlocks down to his yellow Nike running shoes.

"What we got, Sister Ro Ro?"

"Somebody put two into Al O'Grady. Bart found him."

"Hmmm. Al was a good dude. Let me get to work so I can decipher this riddle."

Rowena pointed to the row of stools. "One of those stools is out of synch. See if you can help this Blond figure out why."

Bart smirked. "Typical Ro Ro. She just loves to make a mystery out of a miscue."

"Murder is not a miscue," she snapped.

Docky waved a finger under Bart's nose. "Don't piss her off Bart. She owns a broadsword I am told."

Rowena grinned as she made a chop motion across the front of Bart's pants. She took Bart by the arm. "Come with me. I need a statement."

"Sure thing."

Rowena glanced at the out of place stool. What could it mean? Bart's statement shed no light. He'd worked all night on a car-jacking of a female Uber driver that turned into a rape case. It seemed he had an alibi. And needing a bourbon after an all-nighter was understandable. But she would verify his story with the precinct officers. She called the Records Department and got the address and phone number of Germanton John Mancuso.

He answered on the fourth ring.

"This is John."

"Mancuso. This is Officer Rowena Morse. I am coming to pay you a visit regarding the shooting death of Al O'Grady. I will be there in fifteen minutes."

"Take your time. I ain't leaving town. Sorry about O'Grady. Owning a bar is a dangerous occupation."

Rowena shook her iPhone like she was wringing his neck. "Yeah. So is bookmaking, loan sharking, and murder. Do not leave your residence."

Mancuso chuckled. "I like feisty dames. Come over, please."

Rowena hung up. G Town's impunity rankled her. She had to control her anger before she gave in to the temptation to pistol whip the arrogant bastard.

Chapter Two

*G*ermantown John lived in a hundred-year-old, two-story stone home on West Gravers Lane in Chestnut Hill, a short ride up the trolley tracks and cobblestoned Germantown Avenue. The "Hill" is a town within the city. A vigilant community association scrutinizes all new store openings, renovations, and building projects.

The Hill's newspaper prints weekly and reports on all things Chestnut Hill. Ro Ro wondered how a low life Germantown hood like G Town John was allowed to join the civilized gentry of the Hill.

He agreed to see her sans lawyer. Was he being macho or was he just showing her scorn? She relished being underestimated.

She found a parking spot four houses away under a tall maple tree. An elderly man dressed in baggy shorts and a faded University of Pennsylvania red and blue tee shirt walked past her, eying her warily.

He probably thinks I am a hooker who made a wrong turn. Ro Ro got out of the car, badge in hand. "Excuse me Sir. I am Detective Morse. May I ask you a question?"

The man stared at her badge and her breasts with equal interest. "Sure Dear. My name is Gordon Shuster. I live two doors down the street."

Ro Ro winced at the word "Dear." Condescendence annoyed her. "Do you know Mister John Mancuso?"

Shuster's bony fingers rubbed his gray chin stubble. "Oh, you mean the dago. He's a bit sleazy. People come and go to his house at all hours. Is he a mobster like on the Sopranos?"

"Tell me more about his visitors."

"Well, there is a short guy who was here last night. And then there is a red-haired man who wears a fedora. I noticed because I wear one myself. And there is also a fancy dresser. Always wearing suits even in the heat. Maybe he's a lawyer."

Little Tony, Jumper, and Bart. All on Germantown John's visitor list.

"Wait Officer. I saw the television story about that bar owner who was shot. He was here last week."

Rowena held back a gasp. "When exactly was he here?"

Shuster was now staring openly at her chest. Ro Ro wanted to slap him.

"Tuesday. I remember because I play Mega Millions and I hit the Mega ball for two whole dollars. I never win those darn things." Rowena gave him her card. He cradled it like she had given him a winning lottery ticket.

"Please keep an eye on Mancuso and call me if and when any of these men reappear. Will you do that for me?"

"Sure will."

Rowena gently squeezed Shuster's arm as if to seal their deal.

"Thank you, Mister Shuster."

"Call me Gordy," he smiled like a school kid at a sophomore hop.

"And you can call me Officer Morse."

Gordy's smile evaporated.

Rowena turned on her heel as she headed towards G Town John's house. Her nostrils flared in anger. Bart had lied to her. Bastard. John Mancuso was the son of a brick layer who spent Saturday's losing more than half his paycheck at Garden State race track. By the time John reached sixteen, he'd learned it was more profitable to take bets as a bookie than try to pick winners. He never bet on an unfixed race. He made his bones by taking out one of Gang Boss Joey Merlino's assassins in a knife fight.

High hedges surrounded Casa Mancuso like a natural barrier. She scaled the six steps to a wooden porch where a hammock hung from the wooden porch ceiling. A hand-written note "Out Back" was pinned to the oak wood front door. She tracked along a cement walk, noting that the side of the house was shielded by hedges as well.

Luscious red ripe tomatoes hung along a dozen stakes. Mancuso sweated under a broad straw hat. A sleeveless tee shirt clung to his hairy chest. His long, muscular legs stretched to his low-cut Nikes. His biceps bulged like a man who did chin ups for a living. He turned and flashed a broad, sexy smile, his blue eyes alight as the Summer sky.

Rowena and Mancuso's eyes locked. She sensed he was testing her, sizing up her mental strength.

"Hello Mister Mancuso. We meet again. I need to ask you questions about the murder of Al O'Grady."

Mancuso nodded. "Sure Detective. Let's go inside. Where is your partner?"

"I have no partner. I work alone."

"Let us go inside."

The kitchen was retro décor stove, fridge, oven, sink, and dishwasher. A water softener was attached to the sink faucet. The appliances gleamed under overhead LEDS. Mancuso took a glass pitcher of iced tea with lemons from the fridge, and two water glasses from the oak cabinets, and set them on a butcher block table.

G Town John was no stereotypical hood, she thought.

Mancuso poured two glasses full. "Enjoy," he said.

Rowena sat opposite Mancuso, mindful that his eyes stayed fixed on hers and not on her body.

"Thanks for the iced tea. Where were you last night?" she said.

"Hah, you go right to the heart of the matter. I like that directness. It does not work with every woman, but you are not typical. Ricky described you as unusual. To answer your question, I stayed home alone last night."

Why did he keep bringing up Ricky?

"So, you have no one who can corroborate that statement?"

"Nope."

"Why were you in O'Grady's bar yesterday afternoon?"

Mancuso held up his left palm and scratched his manicured fingernails across it. "People there owe me money."

"Who owes you money and how much do they owe you?"

"That's confidential."

"In a murder case everything is fair game. Shall I get a warrant to search this house, your tax records, bank accounts, and credit card accounts?"

"Absolutely."

"Why not keep things simple, especially if you did not do the shooting?"

"My business runs on the security of confidentiality. Clients don't want their business put on the street. It's bad all around."

Mancuso swigged his iced tea, stalling, she thought.

"Look Ro Ro, that's what Ricky called you. Anyhow, I want to cooperate because I have nothing to hide regarding who killed Al. If word gets out I caved to the cops and shared certain names, I lose credibility. I will look weak. Then guys will move in on me and I will be dead or broke in a month. That is not a desirable outcome. However, a subpoena gets me off the hook. So, go do your subpoena so you look good, and I will maintain my reputation as a standup guy. Ricky said you had a logical mind, so I am sure you see the logic here."

Rowena nodded, rocking in her hair. "I see your point. Answer me this. Why do you keep bringing my dead ex into the conversation?"

Mancuso refreshed his iced tea. "Ah, that is good tea. My mother used to brew the tea and drop fresh mint leaves in it. God rest her soul. I did not realize I talked about Ricky so much. You see, we were ass hole buddies. I introduced him to Julie Monaco. You know the rest of the story. It's Julie who may have gotten him killed."

Rowena's heart skipped three beats. "What?"

"Ricky could have made that curve on Cresheim Valley Drive with his eyes closed. He was side-swiped into that tree by Julie's ex-boyfriend."

Blood rushed to Rowena's head. Dizzy, she grasped the edges of her chair seat. "Who? Damn it, who?"

Mancuso whispered, "Al O'Grady."

"I do not believe you."

"Make book on it. And if that word gets out, guess who is the prime suspect for killing Al? Y O U." The Police Department will take you off the case and strap your sweet butt to a desk in the basement of the Fourteenth Precinct. I hear the rats there like Brie."

Rowena pounded the table with both fists. "Liar. Liar, Liar."

"Germantown John tells no lies. What is your alibi for last night?"

"You bastard! You lying, conniving bastard."

"Do you want more iced tea?"

Rowena took a deep breath to control her urge to slap G Town across his smiling face. He had her for the moment.

"Mancuso, I am not going to be intimidated by a bullshit artist like you. Expect subpoenas and surveillance. Go tell your lies to whoever is dumb enough to believe them."

"I will. Now get out of my home before I call the cops."

Rowena backed away from G Town's mocking laughter. Her gut told her that the scumbag was telling the truth.

Rowena gunned the engine and headed for the Fourteenth Precinct on Haines Street in Germantown. Her phone rang, so she answered it hands free. Caller ID read, "Lieutenant Jones." Her boss. Jonesy was tall, lean and mean. She'd known him since the eighth grade. He gave her lots of room to operate, but she never crossed the line of taking too much rope lest Harley Jones would come down on her like an avalanche.

"Hello Boss."

"Hello Rowena. What happened with G Town?"

"Lots. I am just leaving his house. I learned a lot that I will report when I get there. Please send officers to pick up Joey the Moocher McKee, Little Tony De Giacomo, and Jimmy the Jumper Roscoe. And please get Docky moving on his report. Mancuso pulled a strong-arm tactic on me. The rats are scared. "

"Good. I can hardly wait to hear your report."

"See you in ten minutes, Boss."

Chapter Three

The hundred year-old brick Fourteenth Precinct building resembles a pre-World War One prison. A black, wrought iron fence separates the building from the run-down houses and empty trash cans in strewn lots on its sides.

The front room serves as a Magistrates Court for DUI and minor offense cases. The Judge holds court from a raised seat, backed by a six foot by six foot American flag.

To the left, police desks and offices are arranged behind secure plate glass protection. The site is simple but safe, non-pretentious.

Harley Davidson Jones, a.k.a. "Biker," welcomed Rowena into his office at the rear with a wave. Biker was a godsend of a Boss. He made sure she was not assigned a partner. Male partners would spend too much effort trying to bed her. Women would spend too much time complaining. "Come In Ro Ro. Tell me about G Town's stunt and how it ties to you."

Biker always dressed like he was going to Church. He sported cuff links daily, usually gold. He despised his nickname, feeling it demeaned his status as a police officer and family man.

Rowena settled into a round back wooden chair. "G Town implied that my ex's car accident was a murder and that I had motive to kill Ricky. The troubling point is that I think he knows something. I want Docky to review the file. Maybe the previous CSU Examiner missed something. Anyway, I think we better be sure there is no way G Town can get me off of this case."

Biker scratched his pencil mustache, a sign he was intrigued. "G Town is slicker than black ice. Okay, I will instruct Docky to check it out since it may be relevant to O'Grady's murder in a roundabout way. What does your gut tell you about the motive for killing Al?" Rowena took a deep breath and sighed, not liking to answer a question when she was not sure of the answer. "At first, I thought it must have been a robbery gone bad, but now I think there is a subtler explanation. I cannot imagine Al being in business with G Town. But Al liked the ponies. He used to say he was going to give me one for Christmas. Now I remember, he gave me a toy palomino pony once as a way of fulfilling his promise. He said the pony was a blond like me. Al was as horny as he was corny. I thought it was a cheap trick into getting me into bed with him. Perhaps my erstwhile knight in shining armor had a gambling problem that tarnished his sword armor. Bars are cash cows and great ways to launder money."

Biker tapped the top of his desk with both fore fingers as if he were typing hunt and peck on a PC. "We will subpoena his bank records and question his CPA or whoever did his taxes."

"Follow the money. The dollars are the bread crumbs that lead you to the truth," said Rowena.

Biker's cell phone buzzed. "Jones," he said. "Good bring him in and then go get the other two losers."

He turned off the phone. "We picked up Little Tony. ETA is ten minutes. Interview him in the rear conference room. It's hot in there. Sweat the punk until the grease soaks his shirt."

Rowena shot him a thumbs-up. "Will do, Boss."

Little Tony De Giacomo barely stood five foot tall. Wiry, well-defined bicep muscles thrust from his black tee shirt, cut sharp from working out at Planet Fitness daily, he had nicknames ranging from Mini Guinea, to Mighty Mouse, to Stub, to Pony Boy. He had a well-deserved reputation as a streetfighter whose first punch was a hard shot to the nuts. He was respected as a crafty bettor on football games. He had a nasty temper and was second cousin to G Town John on his mother's side.

His thick, black hair was slicked back, a retro fifties look, ala Sylvester Stallone, his idol. Rowena likened him to the gargoyles etched in City Hall, only scarier.

He sat across from Rowena, staring at her chest, a smirk twisting from the left side of his mouth.

"Hello Joey," she said purposely avoiding the nicknames.

"Yeah, hello Ro Ro. Bad news about Al. You two were tight."

"Everybody liked Al. He was one of the good guys."

Joey laughed. "Not everybody. Who shoots a friend?"

"A false friend. Why were you in his bar yesterday?"

Joey leaned back. "It was a hot day. I needed a beer."

Funny you and your cousin John show up at the same time. Did Al owe money to G Town?"

"Ask John. I mind my own business."

"You collect for John. Were you guys after Al or Moocher or both?"

Joey's eyes narrowed under his creased brow. "What are you talking about?"

Rowena leaned across the table, staring into Joey's eyes, looking for him to blink.

"Motive. You would cut or shoot Mother Teresa to collect a nickel. Is that why you and your cousin paid Al a visit.?"

Joey held up both hands. "Whoa. Slow down Ro Ro. Joey ain't no killer. I liked Al. He used to call me Short Shot. I called him Tower Man. We were buddies."

Rowena was not about to buy BS from him at any price. "Bull. You were there to send Al a message, not Moocher."

"So how do you figure that?"

"Because Al is dead, and Moocher is alive, Knucklehead."

Sweat beaded on Joey's forehead. "You got it all wrong. Moocher owed eleven large. John wanted him to pay up."

"How much did Al owe?"

Joey's eyes spread wide. "I don't know nothing about Big Al and any debts."

Rowena dug her forefinger into his chest. "Do I have to ask Biker to come in here and reeducate you on getting an ass whipping? Now I ask you again. How much did Al owe G Town?"

Joey flashed ten fingers ten times.

"A hundred large."

"I did not tell you anything. Look at it this way. Let's say Al owed money. Killing him means you are out whatever he owes. Hell, he was the safest man in Mount Airy as far as owing money to John."

Rowena shook a fist under his nose. "Safe? Safe? He was murdered. How safe is that?"

She dropped her voice to a whisper, low and slow for emphasis. Tell me you stupid shit, how safe was Al?"

Joey shrugged, "I guess he was in trouble for some other reason."

Rowena believed Joey may have a valid point. "I like you for killing my old friend. I like you a lot."

Joey leaped up. "Ro Ro. I am clean on this one. I swear."

"Really?"

"Very really. It's too hot in here. I need air."

"Fess up Joey. What do you know that you are not telling me? If I catch you holding back, I will swat you like a sick fly."

Joey's chest heaved, his face turned sheet white. "Ro Ro. You got to believe me. I know nothing more."

"Believe you? Hah. I'd believe the devil before I believe you. Get out but do not leave Philly. I am declaring you a material witness in a murder investigation. Got it?"

Joey backed away. "Got it Ro Ro."

Biker entered, smiling as Joey scurried down the hallway and out of the Precinct.

"You lit a bonfire under his ass. He'll be running like a greyhound to G Town."

"There is a lot more to this story. I don't think I am going to like the truth when I find it."

Docky filled the doorway looking troubled. "Hey Miss Ro Ro. Why do you want me to go chasing your dead old man's ghost when I got to figure out what happened to Al?"

Rowena told him about her visit with G Town.

"Now I get it. That G Town is highly likely to have filled my slab with more than one body. You look tired. Best rest up if you are going to tangle with G Town. That man is evil. I would give my false teeth to nail his butt."

"If he killed Al or had him killed, I'll nail him, and you can keep your choppers. I am going home to shower and lie down for a think session. Call me when you bring in the next turkey."

Rowena lathered her body under the warm shower water. Usually a shower soothes her, but her mind was running in circles. Her world was in chaos and the eerie feeling that her past was about to rise from the grave unnerved her.

She slipped on an old pair of cotton pajama bottoms and a Phillies tee shirt and crawled under the covers. After Ricky died, she avoided men, feeling that a good-looking widow was an easy target for lechers. She had a brief affair with a charming, divorced businessman who escorted her to England and Scotland. The tryst with Bart was a moment of weakness brought on by loneliness. She had the job and her friends but no children, no legacy except for her record of finding murderers. Problem solving of the first degree, a

90

skill worthy of the best mathematicians.

Her cell rang.

"Hello Biker. What's up?"

"We brought in the Moocher."

"I will be there in twenty minutes. Put him in the hot room. No water."

"Guantanamo style."

"Reverse water boarding."

"You are too freaking much."

Rowena dressed quickly. She was tempted to take five minutes to row the Chuck Norris gym, but she was more worried about her case than her physique.

Moocher owed a lot of money to G Town and probably others including the hundred bucks she lent him at Christmas. Why did Al stick his neck out for a known loser? It was a bad gamble. Or was it a payoff?

She called Biker from her hands free. "Boss. It is me. I changed my mind on how to approach Moocher. When Moocher gets there offer him soda, maybe a Tastykake too. I want him relaxed and thinking he is among friends. This is one rat who likes honey as much as he likes money."

"Seduction, eh? Why not."

"Call it persuasion."

"Hah. Now you are Miss Congeniality with a badge."

"I like Lady Macbeth better."

"Figures. The schmooze is on."

"Have you located Jumper?"

"Nope. We will get his worthless butt in here."

"I'm counting on it."

Chapter Four

*J*oseph Emmet (Moocher) McKee was the seventh child of eight McKee children. The other seven were all girls so Joey was a true Irish Prince. The only thing he did in the way of a chore was to bring in the mail from the mail slot in the front door of their row home and deposit it on the dining room table. Work and ambition were equal strangers to Joey.

By the time he reached eighth grade, he had developed his gift for weaseling favors and money from friends and neighbors. He'd borrow money promising his friends that he would bet on only a sure thing and his friends would get his money back and half the profits. No one ever recalled getting a payback.

Now in his mid-fifties, Joey had patriotic eyes, blue eyeballs over the white space, surrounded by a bright red rim, compliments of daily shots of Jameson and John Powers Irish whisky.

Luggage-sized bags drooped from his bleary eyes to his cheek bones. He made beagles look suave.

Growing up, Rowena and Joey lived on the same block, walked to Holy Cross grammar school together, and shared gossip and secrets. He tried to kiss her once. She let him but when his hand squeezed her breast, she kneed him in the nuts, sending him rolling on the ground. All seven of his sisters thanked her.

Rowena found Moocher sitting comfortably at the table, gnawing on a soft pretzel, mustard lining his thin lips. He greeted her with a burp. "Oops. Sorry Ro Ro. Mustard gets my innards in a ruckus, but I cannot eat a soft pretzel without a dab of mustard."

She held off a retort about how he gave her the yips.

"No problem. Do you want Grey Poupon?"

"Poop on what?"

"Never mind. We are here for Al. It is a tragedy and a mortal sin against all of us."

Moocher stuffed the end of the pretzel in his mouth just above the gaping hole in his lower front teeth. He chewed away, drooling.

"Sure. T'was a terrible thing with somebody murdering Al. He was good guy. Have you any idea who did it?"

"We are working the case from all angles. How much do you owe G Town John?"

Moocher chewed slowly, avoiding her question. "Got a mouthful."

"Take your time. We have a lot of time. Five years for withholding evidence and obstruction of justice."

Moocher rolled his eyes. "Boy o boy. You sure can ruin a good pretzel. I owed Al ten large. He paid off G Town. T'was Jumper who owed G Town big time."

"So, you had ten thousand reasons to kill Al?"

Moocher thumbed his chest. "Me? Slow down to a trot. I ain't got the balls to kill a mouse. "

"Why did Al buy you out?"

Moocher shuffled his black high-top sneakers making a squeaking sound that sent a shiver up Ro Ro's arms.

"I dunno," he said.

"Bullshit. Fess up Joey. Tell me why Al stuck his neck out for you." Moocher leaned over the table. "You got to keep this hush hush. Al took up with my sister Joan."

"Joan is a freaking nun and she weighs two hundred if she weighs an ounce."

"Beneath the habit she's got all the goods you have."

Ro Ro blanched as an image of Joan and Al copulating rolled across her mind.

"How long has this unholy affair been going on?"

"Years! She gets birth control from Planned Parenthood in Germantown at their office on West Chelten Avenue. Now maybe you understand I had no reason to kill Al. He was my banker and Joan was the collateral."

Rowena laughed, "Moocher my man. You got more scam in you than P.T. Barnum. Tell me, who do you think shot Al?"

Moocher scratched his chin as if contemplating the origin of dark matter. "T'aint scarcely sure but I think your old beau Black Bart may have an inkling. Word on the street is that he found Al, but I also heard Bart owed Al and G Town beau coup cabbage. May hap fifty grand."

Rowena clenched her fists ready to smash Bart square in his mouth. "Joey, if you are lying, I will kick your nuts so hard they will wrap around your ears."

Moocher crossed his hands over his lap. "You got me once. I ain't going for twice. I told you the truth as sure as the sun rises in the East and sets in the West."

She was afraid to believed him.

"Tell me how Bart Malone fits into this picture."

"Whoa. Now you are asking me to chime the bell on a cop. That's a horse of a different color. Besides, he was your boyfriend, wasn't he? You should know about the people you keep company with."

"Lectures from you on behavior are less than credible. So, cut the bullshit and tell me how Bart Malone ties into the bookmaking operation run by G Town John."

Moocher smiled like he'd just found a hundred-dollar bill on the sidewalk. "Miss Smart Panties doesn't get it. Al had his own set up. Bart was his cover, his police protection. Al ran numbers, lent money at high rates and made book on all sports. And Bart got a piece of the action. None of this sat well with G Town John."

Rowena waited until the revelation set in that Al was dirty, and Bart was dirtier. "So when G Town visited Al's bar, who was he looking to send a message to?"

Moocher whispered, "Jumper Roscoe. He wed G Town. My guess is that Jumper shot Al to pay off his debt to G Town. With Al out of the picture, G Town had the whole megillah. Mount Airy, Germantown, and Chestnut Hill. Maybe some of Montgomery County too. Wyndmoor for sure. You got to keep me out of this. If G Town finds out I mentioned his business, I will be eating soft pretzels with Al."

"So why are you telling me all of this?"

"Life Insurance. If you dress G Town John in an orange suit, I get a freebie on the debt and I feel a lot safer. I got an allergy to bullets." Biker opened the conference room door, his brows furled. "Good news. We found Jumper. The bad news is that he shot himself and left a note confessing to shooting Al O'Grady."

"Holy shit," said Moocher.

Rowena shook her head from side to side. "No way Jumper killed himself. Please get Docky on the job. I've got to go see an old friend."

"Can I skedaddle now?" asked Moocher.

"Yes, but I may have more questions for you later. No road trips, you hear?"

Moocher backed out the door and shut it behind him.

Rowena speed dialed Bart Malone.

"What's up Ro Ro?"

"Jumper is dead. Come to the Station, Bart. I have new evidence we need to discuss. Hurry. I need you."

"Sure thing. I will be right there."

"What are you up to?" asked Biker.

"Did Docky review Ricky's case?"

"Yes, he did. A copy is on your desk along with the CSU report on Al's murder. You read them first, then tell me what's going on." Ro Ro speed read the report on her ex's death in four minutes, memorizing each word as if they were implanted into her brain.

"The officer who found Ricky dead behind the wheel was Bart Malone. That is how I met Bart."

"Connect the dots," said Biker.

"I always do, Boss. Now I need to read Docky's report."

"What are you looking for?"

"The most elusive thing in the world. The Truth."

Chapter Five

$\mathcal{R}$owena Isabella Morse was raised Roman Catholic by two staunch Catholics, Desmond and Hannah, who believed the Pope was infallible, sex was sinful, non-Catholics were doomed to hell, and females had no need to go to college.

She attended Holy Cross, a Catholic grade school and Cardinal Dougherty, a Catholic High School. She lost her religion before she lost her virginity. An expose' on pedophile priests named six priests from Cardinal Dougherty. Rowena reasoned that such men could not put God in a person's mouth. When she commented to her father, he swatted her with the back of his hand, splitting her lip.

She vowed no man would ever again get away with hitting her. Ricky had broken her heart by cheating on her and making a fool of her. The only good thing he did was die from natural causes and leave her ten thousand dollars, enough to help her get an Associate's degree at Community College of Philadelphia with a Major in Criminal Justice. The degree helped her career. And Bart Malone helped her get the insurance money. Without it she may have been a Walmart greeter for life. She owed him big time. She was about to pay him back. Maybe.

Bart sauntered into the conference room, smiling as if he hit the Powerball lottery.

"Hey Ro Ro. What's up Buttercup?"

"My blood pressure is soaring, Sit down. We need to talk," she said.

Bart saw the case file for Richard Rawlings. His smile faded to black.

"Why are you looking at that old case?"

Rowena tapped the file, "I like history. When Ricky bought it you were the detective of record. You convinced the CSU to declare the cause of death to be a heart attack. In fact, Ricky was bombed out of his mind. His drunkenness would have negated any insurance claim. They could have claimed contributory negligence, or suicide. You falsified the report to help me. Right?"

"Yes. I liked you and felt sorry for you. And I would do it again for you. I had feelings for you and still do."

Rowena crossed her arms and sat back. "Wrong! The report photos show marks of a side swipe by a white car on the passenger side. Police cars are painted white. You side swiped Ricky and covered it up. You convinced the CSU to ignore the dent, saying it was to protect me. You used me, didn't you?"

Bart slammed his fist onto the table. "No. You got it wrong! Hey, Ro Ro, you got the money not me. Maybe you had him run into that tree? Maybe you killed him for the insurance money or had someone do it for you?"

"Look Bart. This conversation is off line. There is no microphone on or tape rolling. Who killed Ricky and who knew the truth?"

Bart looked away, staring at the blank far wall. "You are off base. I don't know what you are talking about. This is like fake news. How can you believe this cockamamie theory?"

"Why does the truth scare you so much? I am going to repay the money and reopen Ricky's case. He was a jerk, but he did not deserve to be murdered."

Bart walked around the table, avoiding her gaze. He stopped pacing and leaned down by her shoulder. "It was an accident. We were both whacked on gin. Evil stuff that gin. We drag-raced but I misjudged the curve and barely nudged him into that tree. I can still see his eyes staring at me in disbelief. I am sick about it. Sick to my stomach. Can't we just let it go?"

"How do I let it go?"

Bart sat next to her, clutching her hand. "Forgive me Ro Ro. I am a weak man. I am weaker than a child."

"You are a child. Just resign. Get out. Or give me the truth about Al O'Grady's murder. Why was Al shot? Was it a hit? Did you do it?"

Bart squeezed her hand. "I did not kill Al. I swear to Christ in heaven I did not do it."

Rowena pulled her hand away, reached in her briefcase and pulled out Docky's report on Al's shooting. She turned to page three. "Read Docky's comments. He dusted the bar stools and found boot prints. Guess whose?"

Bart read the notes. "I'll be damned. The dumb ass should have posted his picture on Facebook and wrote that he had killed Al."

"Bring him in and I will forget the other report. And I mean alive."

"Okay. I will do it."

Bart left, unaware that Biker was trailing him.

Rowena needed a Margarita, but she settled for a Keurig dark roast coffee no sugar, no cream. A weight was off of her shoulders.

Chapter Six

*D*ocky trundled along the Formica floor carrying a third report on Jumper Roscoe.

"Here Miss Ro Ro is the initial take on Mr. Roscoe. He was shot with the same gun as was Al O'Grady. Was not a suicide. Hell. Ray Charles could see it was murder."

"Thanks, Docky, "

"Have you arrested the fool?"

"I sent Bart to arrest him."

"Who is gonna arrest Bart?"

"Biker, if Bart gets cute."

"That chair being out of line was the key. How did you figure that out?"

"Call it feminine logic. I knew Al would never clean up and leave a chair out of line. Ergo, someone else handled the chair. Simple algebra works. And that man was the killer," she said.

Docky patted her shoulder. "Yeah. Joey used the chair to disguise the angle of the shot and his height, so we would be looking for a man of a different height. Smart idea but dumb execution. Knuckleheads are everywhere,"

"I wonder who gave him the idea?"

Rowena called Biker. "Where is Bart?"

"He went right to G Town's house. Little Tony is there. Bart is taking Little Tony out in cuffs. He's putting Little Tony in the car. Tony looks like he is coked up. I'll stay on him. Oh shit! Bart just shot Tony. I am going in. Send the back up."

"Damn!" said Ro Ro. "He was always dirty."

She heard shots fired. "Biker! Biker! Talk to me Biker. Are you alright?"

"Yeah. Bart never could shoot straight. I brought him down. Get Docky out here."

Rowena rushed to her car and sped to G Town John's home. She had tested Bart and he had failed. He'd murdered Ricky as sure as Little Tony stood on a bar stool in his sneakers and shot Al while Bart watched him, guiding him through the murder. When Bart saw the report identifying Little Tony, he knew he had to shoot him. Jumper was the stooge. And G Town had planned it all.

She found G Town sitting on a bench in his back yard, a glass of red wine in hand. He wore a straw hat with a red, white, and green band. "Welcome nice boobs. There was quite a scene out there today. Lots of shoot them up, cops and robbers stuff. Want some dago red?"

Ro Ro walked behind him and slapped the back of his head. "Damn fly was about to bite you."

G Town rose up, his chest heaving, his eyes narrowed like a cobra ready to strike, "You bitch."

"I am not done with you Johnny Boy. You will slip up someday and I will chop you down like a dead tree."

"Yeah, sure. You will get yours."

"Why did you kill Ricky?"

"He got out of line. I had to teach him a lesson."

"I see. Go play with your tomatoes. But just remember, Ro Ro Morse will get you as sure as God made little green tomatoes."

*D*ressed in sweat pants, a tee shirt, no bra, and low-cut shoes, Rowena pushed herself extra hard on the home gym. Harder, faster, stronger. She had to get in shape for the long haul. She had to bring down Germantown John.

Over her shoulder, Janis Joplin sang her signature ballad, "Piece of My Heart."

Janis was strong, defiant in her love. You could break her heart but not defeat her.

"No one will ever break my heart again," said Ro Ro. "No one."

Epilogue

*T*he full Summer moon cast a pale over the tomatoes; their sheen promised G Town John a tasty tomato salad, drenched in olive oil and mixed with thin sliced onions and peppers and a sprinkle of garlic and oregano. Fresh Amorosa rolls from the South Philly Bakery to mop up the juice. And a glass of dago red to wash it down.

G Town puffed on his Dominican cigar, savoring the fruits of a good day's work.

His throwaway cell buzzed.

"Yo Boss," said Biker.

"Hello Harley. You did well today."

"Yeah. I did not mind shooting that pompous-ass Malone. I made the world a better place. When do we take over O'Grady's bar?"

G Town did not like Biker, but he was useful. "My bank will call the note and cash in the life insurance policy he turned over to the bank. We own the business and the bricks. You will see your twenty percent cut in the Swiss Account in two months. Has Rowena any clue she's helped us?"

"Nah. That is the main reason I do dot assign her a partner. A partner would complicate things. It is best to let her think she is special and old Biker is her best friend."

"For her sake, she better not catch on," said G Town.

"Right. Nice doing business with you," said Biker.

G Town hung up. He plucked a ripe tomato, wiped the skin with his hands, making it shine. He bit into the tomato. Juice drizzled down his chin.

Sweet and luscious, like Rowena, he thought, and ripe.

To be continued ...

Ode to Janis
–A piece of our heart–

She lived in her voice, bluesy, kind
Her soul wrapped in melodic cries
A lilting, mournful, childish whine
For love amid bourbon and pills.

The crowd caught her raw, raspy songs
Her tender, fierce, knowing, wiry strains
That tied singer to listener in bonds
Of heart, soul, and tortured mind.

She died alone in murky haze
Her voice stilled, chilled in icy time,
Yet resurrected in new ways
Her passion and pain breathing anew.

Good night sweet, lonely princess.
We hear your plaintive woe,
We celebrate the art of Janis
Forever a piece of our pulsing heart.

www.ingramcontent.com/pod-product-compliance
Lightning Source LLC
Chambersburg PA
CBHW051515260626
47162CB00008B/2975